MAKING CHANGE HAPPEN

A BLUEPRINT FOR DEALING WITH CHANGE IN 8 SPHERES OF LIFE

DIPESH MA

BlueRose ONE
Stories Matter
New Delhi • London

BLUEROSE PUBLISHERS
India | U.K.

For permissions requests or inquiries regarding this publication,
please contact:

BLUEROSE PUBLISHERS
www.BlueRoseONE.com
info@bluerosepublishers.com
+91 8882 898 898
+4407342408967

ISBN: 978-93-93384-77-5

Cover design: Muskan Sachdeva
Typesetting: Rohit

First Edition: August 2023

PREFACE

In "Making Change Happen," I, Dipesh Majumder, share my personal and professional experiences of navigating change and turning those into opportunities. Growing up in a small town in northeast India, moving to the south of India for higher studies, building multiple businesses, turning from an entrepreneur to an employee, and hustling at present - change has been the only constant for me.

Traveling for work internationally has been a great learning experience. I was lucky to see how people deal with life and business challenges in different cultural contexts. I have applied my experience combined with distilled knowledge gained from books and my mentors to the work setting and life in general to become a change agent. Some concepts presented in this book are fundamental and probably you'd know already, some will act as reminders and nudges while the remainder would be fresh insights. I promised to arm you with practical no-fluff ideas, concepts, tools, and trackers so that you can understand and implement how to deal with change and how to make it work in your favor.

Throughout the book, I have shared my insights and strategies to deal with change, including the importance of empathy and kindness, the power of a customer-centric approach in business and work, and the value of a growth mindset. I also share my experience of losing my mother after a long medical struggle, and how it inspired me to reignite my passion to solve healthcare problems in India. My curiosity about anthropology has also taught me to appreciate diversity and different perspectives, which has been valuable in my personal and professional life.

In this book, I will provide you with various tools, frameworks, and resources such as workbooks, trackers, and planners to help identify and overcome barriers to change. While some of these tools may require a cost, I will also suggest free alternatives. Use them as a guide and choose the best option based on your availability of time, money, and effort.

This book is designed to be flexible and easy to navigate, allowing you to jump to specific chapters as needed. It can be used as a standalone resource or as a reference guide. My goal is for it to serve as a catalyst for reflection and growth, and to be a valuable resource that you will return to time and again.

"Making Change Happen" is a must-read for anyone looking to bring change in their personal or professional life. I offer a unique perspective and practical advice on how to navigate change in the eight spheres of life. My book doesn't claim to be an encyclopedia, instead, it provides guidance on how to tackle common challenges that arise in each of the 8 spheres of life. I hope that readers will take the useful insights and apply them to other problems they may be facing, which may not be covered in the book. This book is an actionable guide that I wrote intending to inspire and empower individuals to make change happen.

TO MY MAA, PRAMILA

It is with great honor and a heavy heart that I dedicate this book to my dear mother, Pramila Majumder. I launched the book cover on the 1st anniversary of my mother's death. One year ago, we lost her to this world, but her legacy and memory live on through the love and wisdom she imparted to me and to so many others.

My mother was a woman of great strength and perseverance. She faced many challenges in her life, but she always found a way to overcome them with grace and determination. She taught me the importance of hard work, commitment, and never giving up on your dreams.

As I wrote this book on navigating change and making positive changes in one's life, I couldn't help but think of my mother and the many changes she faced in her life. She always approached change with a positive attitude and a willingness to adapt and grow. She was an inspiration to me and hundreds of her students who still reach out to seek her for advice and good wishes, only to learn of her untimely demise. It is my hope that this book will serve as a reminder of my mother's legacy and the lessons she taught me. I believe that by following the advice and strategies outlined in this book, readers will be able to make the changes they want to see in their lives.

I hope this book offers a unique perspective on navigating change in your personal and professional life. It is not just a collection of theoretical concepts, but a practical guide that you can apply to your life. Additionally, I believe I am still traveling and have not arrived at any destination in life. Hence, I am co-learning, co-hustling, and co-building with my readers. By choosing to invest in this book, you will gain valuable insights and strategies from someone who faced the same doubts, frustrations, and disappointment with strategies to overcome them to make change happen in your own life.

THANK YOU

I wanted to take a moment to express my deepest gratitude and appreciation for the guidance, support, and inspiration of my mentors. Your wisdom and teachings have been invaluable to me, and I am forever grateful for the positive impact you have had on my life.

I would like to particularly thank John C. Maxwell, Guy Kawasaki, Darren Hardy, Sadhguru, Vishen Lakhiani, Dale Carnegie, and Brian Tracy for the books, speeches, and teachings which have been a constant source of inspiration and motivation for me, and I am eternally grateful for the lessons and insights you have shared over the years.

My father and role model in many ways, Dilip Majumder, thank you for being a shining light in my life, and for helping me to become the best version of myself. Your contributions directly and indirectly to my personal and professional growth are immeasurable and I will be forever grateful for your guidance.

I would also not like to miss the opportunity to thank my school friend and now wife, Jayashree for the tremendous support & guidance. It's so enjoyable to grow old and navigate this mad world together!

Love and hugs to Divit and Joel - both of you complete us!

INTRODUCTION

This book is not meant to be a mere decoration on your bookshelf. It's meant to be used, to be put into action and not just read!

Winners learn HOW to quit DOING the wrong things at the RIGHT time. They learn how to make tough decisions and take the necessary steps to achieve their goals.

Let's face it - life is hard, and it's not always rainbows and butterflies. Positive outcomes and negative outcomes both come with their own set of challenges. Exercise is hard, but so is hospitalization. Marriage is hard, but so is divorce. Entrepreneurship is hard, but so is living with regret. We have a choice to make - we can either lead our lives in the direction of success or in the direction of failure. We need to accept the fact it is hard both ways.

What's effortless to do can be just as effortless to neglect. It's a simple concept that's often missed. We might find it simple to get lost in social media, binge-watch Netflix, or put off tasks, but it's equally effortless to ignore activities that promote our wellbeing and help us reach our goals.

Before the era of the internet, knowledge was seen as a precious resource. Rulers would dispatch their trusted counselors on long, perilous journeys to gather fresh insights. In contrast, today's digital world provides an abundance of information on virtually any subject at our fingertips. The challenge lies not in identifying what needs to be changed but rather in implementing the change itself. This is where many stumble, despite having ample knowledge.

I have seen people change when they're hurt enough, learn enough, or receive enough from life. Transformation is not an easy process, but it's necessary for growth.

The crucial question to ask yourself is this: are you merely interested in change, or are you fully committed to it? Interest is fleeting, and your mind may try to come up with all sorts of excuses to keep you comfortable and safe in your current situation.

However, any change that leads to self-improvement has one thing in common - it requires stepping out of your comfort zone and embracing discomfort.

We have to remember, growth and success are often found just outside of our comfort zone, and the rewards of making positive changes in our lives far outweigh the temporary discomfort we may experience. So, are you ready and willing to be uncomfortable and stay committed to creating a better version of yourself?

While change might decrease efficiency at first, persistence can boost efficiency in the long run. That's why commitment is vital. It ensures that you persist with necessary tasks, even on days when motivation lags.

Therefore, it's essential to choose your changes wisely and make decisions that will improve your health, wealth, love, and lifestyle. By committing to these changes, you can gradually increase your efficiency and make progress towards your goals.

Improvement requires change. This change can either originate from within ourselves or from feedback we receive from others. Are you willing to seek feedback in order to bring about change? Once you've identified what needs to change, the real work begins - it's all about executing and getting it done.

No one can guarantee success or failure, but one certain thing is change. Whether we choose to change or not, life will bring about changes that can either make us or break us. The choice is ultimately in our hands, and it's up to us to make that choice now or risk losing the opportunity.

Change is inevitable, but suffering is optional. Let's embrace change and use it as an opportunity for growth and self-improvement, rather than letting it cause unnecessary pain and hardship. Are you ready to take the next step in becoming the best version of yourself?

In this book, we will discover how making positive changes in the 8 spheres of life can truly transform you. From improving your health and wealth to enhancing your relationships and lifestyle, the possibilities are endless. Let's dive in and start the journey toward self-improvement together.

CHAPTERS

Chapter 1: Business and Change

The chapter on Business and Change discusses the challenges that organizations face when implementing change. It explores issues such as resistance to change, lack of clear communication and direction, insufficient resources, difficulty adapting to new technologies and processes, and the importance of measuring the success of the change.

Chapter 2: Finances and Change

This chapter offers practical tips on how to plan and manage finances during various life changes, such as adapting to changes in the economy, early parenthood, the digital age, and the effect of job loss. We will learn strategies for adapting financial plans to changing circumstances and navigating financial changes effectively.

Chapter 3: Relationships and Change

This chapter highlights the importance of embracing change in relationships. It covers managing change when moving in together, adapting to change over time, balancing independence and connection, and managing the impact of technology on relationships.

Chapter 4: Physical and Change

This chapter explores the various ways physical health affects our well-being, including the impact of weight, chronic illness, technology, sleep patterns, and aging. Learn how to adapt to physical changes and navigate them gracefully to lead a healthy life.

Chapter 5: Mental and Change

This chapter discusses the psychological impact of different types of change in life. It covers topics such as managing trauma, supporting family mental health, navigating loneliness in the digital age, coping with relocation, and navigating breakups and divorces.

Chapter 6: Spiritual and Change

This chapter highlights the consequences of ignoring the spiritual aspects of change and how it can lead to stagnation in life. It emphasizes achieving holistic transformation by incorporating the mind-body-spirit connection and spiritual principles for effective leadership during times of change.

Chapter 7: Family and Change

The chapter explores the challenges and opportunities that modern families face in the digital age, as well as the changing role of gender and sexuality in family life. It also discusses how families can embrace diversity and support elderly family members through transitions while balancing tradition and innovation.

Chapter 8: Lifestyle and Change

In this chapter, we learn how to transform our lifestyle by intentionally designing and planning our life to align with our passions, breaking the cycle of procrastination, and rewiring limiting habits for personal growth and change through self-reflection.

Bonus Chapter:

Embracing Change - A Path to Personal Growth

In the Bonus chapter, we discuss how small, seemingly inconsequential daily choices shape our future profoundly, and how mastering mundane tasks and embracing discomfort is the key to unlocking our full potential. By reflecting on our priorities, creating routines, seeking discomfort, developing a growth mindset, and surrounding ourselves with support, we can achieve remarkable success in every aspect of our lives and make a lasting impact on the world.

This book ends with a small surprise that I hope will delight and inspire you.

Keep reading until the end to discover it!

CONTENTS

1

BUSINESS AND CHANGE

Growing up in a small town, I spent most of my childhood with my grandparents while my parents worked. I listened to stories about my family's experiences during partition and how the Majumders were Zamindars and successful business people in pre-independence India. These stories were a stark contrast to my own humble upbringing and as a child, it was almost too good to believe.

Like any kid, I enjoyed breaking things but what set me apart was my desire to create something new from what was broken. By the time I was a teenager, I had earned the title of "chief destruction officer" and had even burned down our bamboo and tin-shed house while experimenting with fire. I was fascinated by people's reactions to my creations - some encouraged me, others ignored or dismissed me, but only a few gave me genuine feedback.

I was in 9th standard, and by that time my parents built a new house and I had to leave my grandmother's home, it felt like a punishment to me. I spent a year living under their direct supervision before realizing I needed to move away from family and relatives. I greatly valued my independent spirit and wanted to explore and experience things on my own terms. At the age of 16, I decided to move to Chennai instead of more popular options like Bangalore or Delhi.

With nothing stopping me and no interference, I started exploring the city and its people and pace of life. I even started a series of small businesses while studying in college, making enough money to fund my hobbies and launch new ventures one after another.

Being a first-generation businessperson, I understood the importance of perseverance. While many may give up prematurely, I was determined to embrace the journey and take incremental steps. Whether you have a family background in business or not, change is unavoidable, and it's up to you to make the required adjustments for a favorable result. I know you expect a lot from yourself, but sometimes it's important to show yourself kindness in your journey of Business and change.

Some key topics on challenges businesses face when it comes to change

#1. Resistance to change from employees and stakeholders

#2. Lack of clear communication and direction for the change

#3. Insufficient resources (financial, personnel) to implement the change

#4. Difficulty in adapting to new technologies and processes.

#5. Inability to measure the success of the change

#1
Resistance to change from employees and stakeholders

On the Outside:

As a leader, you'll inevitably encounter both types of people in your journey - those who drain your energy and those who inspire and uplift you. People who resist change can be a major source of frustration and stress for leaders. They are often skeptical of new ideas and resistant to new ways of doing things, which can slow down progress and hinder the success of the organization.

When facing resistance from employees and stakeholders, you will feel frustrated, stressed, and like you're not in control. You worry about the negative impact on the business and feel the pressure to find solutions. You also think about the long-term effects on the company if the resistance is not resolved.

"Resistance is not just a hindrance to progress, but also a test of leadership."

- John C. Maxwell

Here's what you will experience on the outside when you face resistance from employees and stakeholders.

Low employee morale and engagement
Negative attitudes and comments toward the change
Lack of cooperation and teamwork
Decreased productivity and performance
Lack of buy-in from key stakeholders
Difficulty in implementing new processes and procedures
High turnover rates / employee churn
Difficulty in achieving desired outcomes
Lack of support from management
Difficulty in achieving the desired level of change adoption.

On the Inside:

Peeling the onion core can reveal its most potent flavor! The layers of the onion represent the visible symptoms of resistance, such as feeling comfortable with current ways, fear of the change's impact, concerns about work-life balance, workload, or relationships with colleagues, and the belief that the change is not in their best interest. I have been an employee and entrepreneur, and I have witnessed firsthand how these factors affect companies when employees resist change.

Understanding the root causes of resistance to change from employees and stakeholders is like peeling an onion. Asking follow-up "why" questions help you uncover the underlying reasons for resistance.

Did you discover any of the following?

- Fear of the unknown and uncertainty, lack of trust in leadership
- Perceived lack of personal or organizational benefit from the change
- Inadequate communication and involvement in the change process
- Perceived loss of power or control
- Loss of job security
- Perceived lack of support and resources
- The perception that the change may not align with company values and culture
- Lack of understanding of the need for change
- Past bad experience with change in the company.

Peeling the onion of resistance allows us to delve deeper into the underlying reasons employees and stakeholders resist change. By understanding these factors, organizations can develop strategies to address concerns, provide support, and gain buy-in, ultimately fostering a smoother transition and successful implementation of change initiatives.

What Decisions do you need to consider?

Throughout this journey, we encountered setbacks and moments of doubt. However, we learned that setbacks are not failures but opportunities for growth and learning. With each challenge, we adapted our approach, leveraging the resilience and determination within us to keep moving forward. We recognized that change is not a linear process, and adjustments were made along the way to navigate unexpected challenges. Each milestone achieved was celebrated, fueling motivation and inspiring us to push forward.

In reflecting on my experience of overcoming resistance to change, I have discovered several effective approaches that proved successful.

Here are some of the strategies that worked:

- Communicate the need for change and its benefits clearly and transparently
- Involve employees and stakeholders in the change process
- Address and mitigate fears and concerns
- Provide training and support for the transition
- Ensure that the change aligns with company values and culture
- Address any potential negative impacts on job security
- Communicate the change effectively and regularly
- Provide opportunities for feedback and input
- Recognize and reward those who support and embrace the change
- Lead by example and demonstrate commitment to the change.

By providing the right care and attention, such as providing the necessary resources, training and clear communication, and addressing the underlying causes of resistance, the workplace can become an environment that nurtures growth.

What results you can hope to see:

Reflecting on the past, it fills me with immense satisfaction to have witnessed the transformative impact we have achieved within my company. We have emerged as a more agile, innovative, and adaptable organization than ever before. Our employees took time but eventually embraced a growth mindset, constantly exploring new avenues to drive success. The alignment of our stakeholders with our vision has been instrumental in fostering a culture that embraces change as a powerful catalyst for progress.

Together, we have laid the foundation for a growth culture within the company and experienced positive outcomes such as:

Increased employee morale and engagement

Higher productivity and performance, cooperation and teamwork

Greater support from employees and stakeholders

More successful implementation of new processes and procedures

Increased ability to achieve desired outcomes

Greater alignment of the change with company values and culture

Improved customer satisfaction

A more adaptive and resilient organization.

As a ball gains momentum, it becomes easier to maintain its motion. Similarly, as employees begin to see the positive outcomes and experience the benefits of change, their resistance gradually diminishes. Recognizing and celebrating small wins along the way reinforces the positive aspects of change and motivates employees to continue embracing it.

Leaders must remain committed, actively listen to concerns, and adjust based on feedback. By addressing resistance with empathy, providing support, and facilitating a culture of continuous learning, even a traditional organization can gradually overcome resistance and foster an environment where change is embraced as a means for growth and progress.

#2

Lack of clear communication and direction for the change

On the Outside:

I have had my share of being part of the good, the bad, and the ugly transformation initiatives. And one thing that stands out time and time again is the devastating impact of a lack of communication on change in business. It's a common scenario: leaders announce a change, employees are left in the dark, and confusion and resistance starts.

When a business lacks clear communication and direction for change, it leads to confusion and uncertainty among employees, making it difficult for them to understand their roles and responsibilities in the change process. This results in decreased productivity and performance, as employees may struggle to adapt to new processes and procedures. Additionally, it damages the relationship between employees, management, and other stakeholders, and negatively impacts the company's reputation.

"*Change without communication is chaos.*"

- Sarah Johnson

Are you experiencing any of the below?

Confusion among employees about their roles and responsibilities in the change process

Decreased productivity and performance

Difficulty in implementing new processes and procedures

High turnover rates or employee churn

Lack of buy-in from key stakeholders

Difficulty in achieving desired outcomes

Damage to relationships between employees, management, and other stakeholders

Negative impact on the company's reputation

Lack of support from management

Difficulty in achieving the desired level of change adoption.

Resistance from employees and stakeholders.

On the Inside:

Going through a business transformation without clear communication is like setting sail without a compass. Without guidance and direction, you risk getting lost and facing resistance from your crew. But when leaders communicate clearly and provide a map for the journey, employees can confidently navigate the change and work together to reach their destination. The lesson? Clear communication is essential for a successful transformation.

"The greatest problem with communication is we don't listen to understand. We listen to reply."

- Stephen Covey

The root cause of the lack of clear communication and direction for change vary depending on the specific situation.

Some common reasons include:

- Insufficient planning and preparation before implementing change
- No clear vision or goals for the change
- No clear communication channels to share the progress and results of change
- No follow-up action on feedback and suggestions from the employees
- A lack of understanding or knowledge about the change among employees and stakeholders
- Poor communication and engagement with employees and stakeholders throughout the change process
- Not involving employees and stakeholders in the decision-making process
- A lack of resources or support from management
- Resistance from employees and stakeholders

TIP: Are you receiving enough feedback from employees and stakeholders? Scan the QR at the chapter end and use one of the survey templates to determine this.

What Decisions do you need to consider?

Drawing from the lessons learned, it is essential to make informed decisions when addressing a lack of clear communication and direction for change.

The following steps have proven effective in improving such situations:

Develop a clear vision and goals: Clearly define the purpose and benefits of the change, and communicate this vision to all stakeholders. Why is more important than how!

Involve employees and stakeholders in decision-making: Encourage participation and collaboration in the change process by involving employees and stakeholders in decision-making, and taking their feedback and suggestions into account. This helps avoid gossiping and rumor-mongering.

Communicate regularly and effectively: Establish clear communication channels and ensure that all stakeholders are kept informed of progress and any changes to the plan.

Provide training and support: Provide training and resources to support employees and stakeholders in adapting to the change.

Monitor and evaluate progress: Regularly track progress and measure performance, and use this information to make adjustments and improvements to the change process as needed.

Address resistance: Identify the root causes of resistance and address them directly. Encourage open communication and provide support for employees and stakeholders to help them adapt to the change.

Provide leadership: Strong leadership is crucial for successful change. Provide clear direction, set an example, and show your support for the change.

TIP: Look for individuals who are open to new ideas and willing to take risks. Often, they are the high performers, innovative thinkers, and future hidden leaders within the organization. They are your early adopters to change.

What results you can hope to see:

Having clear communication and direction is like having a reliable GPS system for our business. It ensures that we know exactly where we're headed and how to get there. Without it, we feel like we're driving blindfolded, relying solely on hope for the best outcomes. But hope is not a strategy, and in the business world, we need clarity to make informed decisions.

Effective communication provides that clarity, guiding us towards our goals with confidence and helping us navigate the challenges along the way. So, it's crucial for us to prioritize clear communication and direction to stay on the right path towards success.

Here's what you can expect to see as key outcomes:

Increased productivity: With clear communication and direction, employees are better able to understand their roles and responsibilities and can focus on their tasks more effectively, leading to increased productivity.

Improved employee morale: Clear communication and direction helps to reduce confusion and uncertainty among employees, which leads to improved morale and engagement.

Better decision-making: When everyone is on the same page and understands the goals and objectives of the organization, decisions are made more effectively and efficiently.

Increased buy-in and support: Clear communication and direction helps to build trust and buy-in among employees and stakeholders, making it easier to implement and sustain change.

Improved customer satisfaction: With clear direction and communication, employees better understand how their work affects the customer, which leads to improved customer satisfaction.

Cost-effective: By providing clear communication and direction, organizations avoid costly mistakes and misunderstandings, which ultimately saves money for the organization.

Better employee retention: Improved morale and engagement leads to lower turnover rates and better retention of top talent within the organization.

Clear communication and direction have become the guiding forces for success, empowering our teams, fostering collaboration, and driving positive outcomes. By prioritizing effective communication, we have unlocked our potential, strengthened relationships, and set the stage for continued growth.

#3
Insufficient resources (financial, personnel) to implement the change

On the Outside:

Change initiatives, much like a game of Jenga, require thoughtful planning and strategy. Just as the goal in Jenga is to delicately remove and place blocks to maintain the tower's stability, leaders facing resource limitations must prioritize initiatives and allocate resources wisely for optimal impact and success. Otherwise, without careful consideration, the tower of change can come crashing down.

"Change is not a matter of resources, but of will."

- Tony Robbins

Insufficient resources, such as a lack of financial and personnel support, hinders a business's ability to effectively implement change. This leads to poor planning, inadequate execution, low employee morale, and ultimately, decreased success in the change initiative and the business.

I found the most common ones below:

Budget constraints: Limited financial resources hinder the implementation of change initiatives.

Shortage of personnel: A lack of personnel limits the ability to carry out the change process effectively.

Delays in implementation: The absence of sufficient resources causes delays in the implementation of change initiatives.

Poor project execution: Inadequate resources leads to poor project execution and a lack of accountability.

Decreased motivation: Insufficient resources reduce the motivation of employees to participate in the change process.

Decreased employee morale: The absence of adequate resources can lead to decreased employee morale and a decrease in job satisfaction.

Inability to achieve desired outcomes: Insufficient resources can hinder a business's ability to achieve its desired outcomes.

On the Inside:

As an Entrepreneur, it is our responsibility to inspire action and empower our employees. However, we must also ensure that our directives to "make it happen" are followed up with proper support and accountability. Insufficient resources, whether financial or personnel, significantly impedes the successful implementation of change initiatives. This resulted in inadequate planning, subpar execution, diminished employee morale, and ultimately, hindered success for both the change initiative and the overall business.

I found the most common root causes as below:

Limited budgetary resources make it difficult to implement change effectively.

Inadequate resource allocation poses a barrier to successful change efforts.

When change initiatives are not prioritized, there may not be enough resources allocated to support them.

Poor planning resulted in a shortage of resources during the implementation phase.

External factors, such as economic downturns, impacted the availability of resources for change.

Resistance to change within the organizational culture restricted the allocation of necessary resources.

By learning from these experiences, I understood the importance of proper planning, proactive communication, and adaptability in overcoming resource constraints and driving successful change efforts.

What Decisions do you need to consider?

With a sprinkle of creativity and a hefty dose of determination, we need to embark on the mission to deal with insufficient resources, fully aware of the precariousness, much like a game of Jenga. The goal is clear: drive change without toppling the tower. It requires a strategic approach, patience, and a steady hand to carefully navigate through the obstacles. It won't be an easy task, but it is possible, and we need to be determined to make it work.

Here are some of the decisions that worked in my favor implementing in real life:

Prioritization: Determine which change initiatives are most critical and align them with strategic goals of the company. Prioritize those initiatives that will have the highest impact and allocate resources accordingly.

Resource allocation planning: Prioritizing and allocating resources effectively, including financial and personnel support, ensures adequate resources are available to implement change effectively.

Resource optimization: Optimizing available resources by streamlining processes, eliminating waste, and maximizing efficiency helps overcome resource constraints.

Employee engagement: Engaging employees in the change process can help mobilize additional resources, including the contributions of their knowledge, skills, and creativity.

Partnership and collaboration: Partnering with other organizations and stakeholders can help pool resources and provide additional support for the change.

Continuously monitor and adjust: Continuously monitoring the situation and adjusting as necessary helped overcome resource constraints and ensured success in implementing change.

These positive changes helped me overcome resource constraints and achieve the desired outcomes and results from the change initiatives. Don't be overwhelmed, scan the QR and I have some quick starter templates for you.

What results you can hope to see:

In project management education, we are taught about the triple constraints and how to address them. However, in the startup world, the constraints are even more pronounced. It is important to understand that having these constraints can be advantageous. I have witnessed projects that have exceeded their budget, timeline, and ultimately been abandoned due to excessive resourcing.

By implementing strategies to effectively manage resources during a change process, businesses can expect to see several positive outcomes, including:

Increased efficiency and productivity: Optimizing available resources and streamlining processes helped improve the efficiency of operations and increase productivity.

Improved employee engagement: Engaging employees in the change process helps to improve morale and increase their commitment to the organization.

Stronger partnerships and collaborations: Forming partnerships and collaborations allowed to leverage resources and expertise, leading to the more successful implementation of change.

Better outcomes: Continuously monitoring and adjusting the change plan made it possible to ensure that the desired outcomes are achieved.

Enhanced reputation and competitiveness: Successfully navigating change, even with limited resources, using lean methods helped build the reputation and competitiveness of the business.

Both as an entrepreneur and an employee, I have realized that by understanding and addressing the root causes of insufficient resources, and by actively managing them, I could set the stage for positive outcomes, foster growth, and achieve success in implementing impactful changes. These learnings have become valuable assets in my professional journey, allowing me to navigate resource limitations with resilience and drive transformative change.

#4
Difficulty in adapting to new technologies and processes.

On the Outside:

As someone who has been fortunate enough to witness the constant evolution of technology since the early 2000s, I have seen firsthand the profound impact it has had on the business environment and workplace. From the rise of smartphones and social media to the transformative power of cloud computing and artificial intelligence, the 5G network, each technological shift has brought about new challenges and opportunities. It is within these changes that individuals and organizations have had to navigate uncertainty and embrace the potential for growth and progress.

"The only way to stay ahead in a rapidly changing world is to embrace change and learn from it."

- Jack Ma

In an organization context, dealing with technological changes can be quite challenging. Here are some of the difficulties

I have witnessed when adapting to these shifts:

Resistance to change: Employees may be reluctant to embrace new technologies and processes, leading to resistance and pushback.

Inefficiency: New technologies and processes needed to be fully understood or adequately implemented. Without this it led to inefficiencies and decreased productivity.

Training and retraining costs: Employees were required to be trained on new technologies and processes, incurring additional costs for the business.

Communication breakdowns: Changes in technology and processes resulted in communication breakdowns between departments and individuals.

Decreased morale: Employees felt overwhelmed or frustrated by the changes, leading to decreased morale and job satisfaction.

Technical issues: Technical problems may arise during the implementation of new technologies, causing delays and decreased productivity.

Loss of expertise: Experienced employees may leave the company due to discomfort with changes, leading to a loss of institutional knowledge and expertise.

Our organizations face numerous challenges when adapting to technological changes, influenced by factors such as rapid advancements, market disruption, regulatory requirements, economic conditions, and societal expectations. Navigating these external factors requires strategic planning, agility, and a proactive approach to successfully embrace and leverage technology for sustainable growth.

On the Inside:

Facing technological change makes employees feel like they're lost in space, floating aimlessly without a sense of direction. This is where businesses need to play the role of the Mission Control, providing clear communication, guidance, and support to help your employees navigate through the galaxy of technological change. With the right training and resources, employees can boldly go where they've never gone before, and thrive in the ever-evolving landscape of innovation.

I found the most common underlying causes as below:

Fear of the unknown: The uncertainty of new technologies and processes led to fear and reluctance to embrace them.

Lack of understanding: Without proper training or education, employees were not fully confident how new technologies or processes work, leading to resistance.

Insecurity about job security: Employees may worry that new technologies will replace their current role or render their skills obsolete.

Resistance to change in general: Some individuals may have a general aversion to change and are resistant to adopting new technologies and processes.

Comfort with current systems: Employees may be comfortable with the current technologies and processes, making it difficult for them to adapt to new ones.

As businesses, we have the power to be the guiding light, igniting the spirit of exploration and innovation within our employees. Let us remember that every great journey begins with a leap into the unknown.

What Decisions do you need to consider?

Let's face it. Change is intimidating, and it's okay to feel scared when things are different. However, change also brings opportunities for growth and excitement. To embrace change positively, it's essential to learn about it, communicate with others, and adopt a mindset focused on personal development. When everyone collaborates and supports each other, change becomes an enjoyable experience, smoothing the transition during the initial stages.

As a business owner or leader, it's your job to:

Emphasize the benefits: Highlight the advantages and benefits of new technologies and processes, and how they will improve work processes and outcomes.

Foster a culture of continuous learning: Encourage employees to continuously learn and develop their skills, and provide opportunities for training and development.

Encourage collaboration and communication: Ensure that employees feel comfortable asking questions and seeking clarification. Encourage open communication between departments to ensure everyone is on the same page and working towards the same goal.

Address concerns and fears: Take the time to listen to employee concerns and address them proactively. Be transparent about the changes and the reasons behind them.

Celebrate successes: Celebrate successes, no matter how small, to boost morale and build momentum towards embracing change.

Provide support: Provide the necessary support and resources to help employees adjust and effectively use new technologies and processes.

Lead by example: As a leader, embrace change yourself and model the behavior you expect from others. This sets a positive example and helps to foster a culture of change.

We hold the key to unlocking the potential within our team. Embrace the benefits that change brings, foster a culture of continuous learning, and create an environment where collaboration and communication thrive. Together, we can conquer our fears, celebrate achievements, and support one another on this journey.

What results you can hope to see:

Our technology-driven society offers tremendous benefits. Consider the transformation of healthcare with healthtech, finance with fintech, and transportation with ridesharing apps. It seems like every major industry now has a -tech suffix, from agri-tech to fashion-tech. The rapid adoption of technology is shaping our future in unprecedented ways. By embracing these changes, businesses can achieve positive outcomes such as enhanced efficiency, better communication, and the ability to innovate and remain competitive.

Some positives are:

Increased efficiency: New technologies and processes streamlines business operations and increase productivity.

Improved communication: Technological changes enhance communication between employees and departments, fostering collaboration and teamwork.

Enhanced customer experience: Technological advancements improve customer service and provide customers with a better overall experience.

Increased competitiveness & innovation: Embracing technology helps companies stay ahead of their competitors and foster growth through the development of new products and services in a rapidly changing market.

Cost savings: Implementing new technologies result in cost savings through automation and improved processes.

Improved decision-making: Access to real-time data and advanced analytics tools provide business leaders with better insights, enabling informed decision-making.

Throughout history, technology has played a pivotal role in shaping our present reality. From the invention of electricity to the rise of the internet, each breakthrough has brought significant changes to our society. As we stand on the cusp of an increasingly digital future, the convergence of technologies like artificial intelligence, blockchain, and renewable energy will shape the world we inhabit. To navigate this future successfully, it is essential to adapt to technological advancements, embrace lifelong learning, and foster a culture of innovation that harnesses the transformative power of technology for the betterment of humanity.

#5

Inability to measure the success of the change

On the Outside:

Oftentimes more than the actual change itself, the lack of measurement of change led me to a state of uncertainty and confusion. You won't know if you should keep using the new method or if you should go back to the old one. It's like trying to bake a cake without a recipe or a timer - you won't know if it's ready or if it's any good!

"If you can't measure it, you can't improve it."

- Peter Drucker

The visible outcomes of the inability to measure the success/failure of a change include:

Poor adoption rates: If employees are not using the new technology or process, it shows that the change was not successful.

Decreased productivity: If productivity decreases after the change, it may indicate that the change was not successful or was not properly implemented.

Increased frustration and resistance: If employees are frustrated with the change and resistant to using it, it tells us that the change was not successful.

Financial losses: This is the worst one. If the change results in financial losses, commercially it is not successful and viable for business.

Poor customer satisfaction: If customer satisfaction decreases after the change, it also proves that the change was not successful or was not properly implemented.

Difficulty in tracking progress: Difficulty in tracking progress is a clear indication that the tracking and measurement mechanisms for the change were not adequately established or effective.

On the Inside:

In my experience with change initiatives, measuring the success or failure of these endeavors has proven to be a perplexing challenge. It has led me to question the underlying reasons behind this difficulty in order to gain a deeper understanding of the issue. By repeatedly asking myself "why," I have been able to peel back the layers and uncover the root causes that hinder accurate measurement.

"In God we trust. All others must bring data."

- W. Edwards Deming

Asking yourself why the inability to measure the success or failure of a change helps us in understanding the root cause of the problem. It also helps us identify any potential obstacles or challenges that may be hindering your progress.

Here are some of my findings:

Undefined or Unclear Objectives: Lack of clear goals and objectives makes it difficult to measure success.

Lack of Measurable Metrics: Inadequate or poorly defined metrics hinder the tracking and evaluation of the change initiative's impact.

Inadequate Data Collection and Tracking: Insufficient data collection systems and processes make it challenging to gather and analyze relevant data.

Timing and Duration of Measurement: Measuring success too early or not allowing enough time for evaluation can result in incomplete or inaccurate assessments.

Lack of Stakeholder Alignment and Engagement: Resistance or lack of support from key stakeholders undermines the ability to measure success accurately.

Complex or Interdependent Factors: Change initiatives involving complex systems or interdependent factors make it difficult to isolate the impact of the change.

Insufficient Resources or Expertise: Limited resources or lack of expertise in measurement and evaluation impede accurate assessment.

Lack of Continuous Monitoring and Evaluation: Inadequate ongoing monitoring and evaluation hinder the ability to make timely adjustments and improvements.

Subjectivity and Perception: Different stakeholders may have varying perceptions of success, making it challenging to establish consensus on measurement criteria.

Organizational Culture and Resistance to Change: A culture resistant to measurement or skeptical of change initiatives can hinder the adoption of effective measurement practices.

In the quest to understand the root cause of the problem, examining the inability to measure the success or failure of a change reveals valuable insights.

What Decisions do you need to consider?

To truly see our organizations, flourish and progress, we need to have clear objectives, well-defined metrics, effective monitoring systems, engaged stakeholders, and a culture that embraces constant improvement. These elements will help us move from a state of uncertainty with no data or visibility to a state of clarity and growth. When measuring the success of a change, it's important to consider both tangible and intangible factors.

Here are some key trackers to help us on our measurement journey:

Performance Metrics: Track specific performance indicators that relate directly to the change, such as sales, customer satisfaction, employee productivity, or process efficiency.

Key Performance Indicators (KPIs): Identify and track the KPIs that are most important to your organization and are directly related to the change.

Cost-Benefit Analysis: Analyze the costs and benefits of the change, both in terms of monetary and non-monetary values. Consider the impact on revenue, expenses, and resources.

Survey and Feedback: Collect feedback from employees, customers, and other stakeholders on the impact of the change. Use surveys, focus groups, or other methods.

Process Improvements: Track process improvements and any other changes to systems, processes, and procedures that resulted from the change.

Employee Engagement: Measure employee engagement, job satisfaction, and morale before and after the change to gauge its impact on the workforce.

Project Management: Use project management tools to track project progress and measure the success of the change initiative against established goals and objectives.

By using a combination of these measurement techniques, we can get a more complete picture of the impact of the change and make informed decisions about future initiatives.

What results you can hope to see:

Through measuring change, we gain visibility into tangible outcomes that enhance our business operations and bottom line.

Personally, I have witnessed the following benefits as a result of measuring change initiatives:

Improved efficiency & increased Productivity: Due to measuring the results of a change and using that to streamline processes and enhance overall productivity.

Better decision-making: With accurate data, as a business leader we can make informed decisions that can positively impact the business.

Increased ROI: By measuring the results of a change, a business leader can now determine if the investment in the change has resulted in a positive return on investment.

Improved customer satisfaction: By monitoring the results of a change, we can determine if the change has had a positive impact on customer satisfaction and make necessary adjustments.

Better planning and forecasting: By measuring the results of a change, as a business leader we can more accurately plan and forecast future business initiatives.

Ready starters for you to start implementing:

(Scan this QR for Mental Models, Links to Proven Frameworks and Excel templates to get started)

2

FINANCE AND CHANGE

My personal relationship with money began at a young age as I served as an eight-year-old accountant for my grandmother's money lending business in Northeast India. This early exposure to finance sparked my interest in the subject and paved the way for my successful career in managing multi-million-dollar client relationships with Fortune 500 companies in the IT services and SaaS product business.

Finance, like all other aspects of life, is an incredibly complex and nuanced field. It is impossible to generalize and summarize its many intricacies. Despite this, finance plays a crucial role in both our personal and professional lives and it is imperative to have a comprehensive understanding of how to navigate it.

In this chapter, I will take you on a journey through my experiences with financial planning, adapting to changes in the economy, managing personal finances, and using change as a tool for financial stability. I will share the lessons I have learned and the tips for success that I have accumulated over the years in the world of finance. My goal in writing this chapter is to provide you with an actionable guide that will inspire and empower you to make changes in your own financial lives. Whether you are just starting out or well-versed with finance, there is something in this chapter for everyone. I will provide insights and advice based on my own experiences, including both my successes and failures, in order to give you an understanding of how finance works hand in hand with other spheres of life.

If you are looking to bring change to your personal or professional life and improve your financial stability, adapt to changes in the economy, or just gain a better understanding of finance, this chapter will provide you with the tools and information you need to make change happen. It's important to remember that this information should not be considered professional financial advice. Always seek out the guidance of a financial advisor for personalized support.

Some key topics on how changes impact your finances

#1. Planning Your Finances Through Change

#2. Adapting to changes in the economy

#3. Managing Financial Change During Early Parenthood

#4. Navigating Financial Change in the Digital Age

#5. Navigating Financial Change due to Job loss

#1
Planning Your Finances Through Change

On the Outside:

Yeah, it's true. Changes, whether they come from outside or within, can often shake up our finances. It could be a change in the economy, a shift in your personal circumstances, or even just a change in your spending habits. The bottom line is, change has a big impact on our money situation.

"Change is inevitable. Growth is optional."

-John Maxwell

Throughout my personal life and business ventures, I've encountered various changes that have disrupted the balance of my finances.

Here are a few examples of these impactful changes:

Financial instability: Without a plan, our finances become unstable during times of change. It is challenging to meet financial obligations, accumulate debt, or handle unexpected expenses.

Missed opportunities: Lack of planning causes us to miss out on valuable opportunities. Whether it's investing in a growing market, taking advantage of low interest rates, or pursuing new career prospects, not having a financial plan may prevent us from seizing these chances for financial growth.

Increased stress: Financial uncertainty leads to additional stress and anxiety. Without a solid plan, we worry about making ends meet, achieving our goals, or dealing with unexpected financial setbacks. This stress impacts our overall well-being and strains our relationships.

Inefficient use of resources: Without a financial plan, we allocate our resources inefficiently. This results in overspending, neglecting important financial goals, or failing to build an emergency fund. As a result, our financial resources may not be effectively used to meet our needs and aspirations.

Inadequate risk management: Unexpected events and risks will arise during times of change. Without proper planning, we are unprepared to handle these risks and protect ourselves financially. This leaves us vulnerable to financial setbacks like job loss, health emergencies, or economic downturns.

Without clear goals and a roadmap, it becomes difficult to measure our financial progress. This slows down our journey towards long-term goals, such as buying a home, startup dreams, saving for retirement, or funding education and so on.

On the Inside:

Dealing with changes in life and business is tough, especially when it comes to finances. If you just react to changes as they happen, you could end up in a real mess. But if you proactively anticipate changes and embrace them, you're much more likely to come out on top. That's why it's important to have a solid financial plan in place, so you're ready for anything that comes your way.

"Ignoring your finances is like driving with your eyes closed."

- Suze Orman

I have witnessed finances undergoing major changes for a variety of reasons, some key reasons include:

Life events: Major life events such as starting a business, getting married, having a child, or dealing with unexpected health events can greatly impact our financial situation.

Economic changes: Changes in the economy such as inflation, recession, or fluctuations in the stock market have a significant impact on our finances.

Unexpected expenses: Unexpected expenses such as home or car repairs, medical bills, or legal fees put a strain on our finances...

Career changes: Career changes such as losing a job, switching careers, or starting a business can have a significant impact on your finances.

Increased debt: Increased debt, whether from loans or credit card balances, puts a strain on our finances and makes it very hard on us to get back on track.

There are a bunch of reasons why you might need to start thinking about financial planning when changes happen in life. Reacting to changes as they happen can lead to messy situations, but by proactively anticipating and embracing changes, we increase our chances of success.

What Decisions do you need to consider?

I've realized the incredible impact that effective financial planning can have on our lives. It can transform our circumstances, provide a sense of security, and set us on the path to a brighter future. The best part is, we don't have to reinvent the wheel! By using proven frameworks and mental models, we can maximize our chances of success, even during challenging times, and maintain a balanced approach to our finances.

To help you on your financial journey, I've curated a list of mental models that I've personally found beneficial.

These models are simple yet powerful tools that can improve your financial well-being and guide you toward success

Mindset of Scarcity vs. Abundance: Consider adopting an abundance mindset, which focuses on growing wealth, instead of a scarcity mindset, which focuses on saving and avoiding debt.

The Pareto Principle: Also known as the 80/20 rule, this principle states that 80% of your results come from 20% of your efforts. In finances, this can mean focusing on high-impact investments or cutting expenses that have the greatest impact on your finances.

The Pay Yourself First Method: This technique involves setting aside a portion of your income each month for savings and investments, before paying any bills or making any purchases.

The Time Value of Money: This model recognizes that money today is worth more than money in the future, due to the effects of inflation and compounding interest. This helps in making an informed decision about when to spend, save, or invest your funds.

The Rule of 72: This rule states that to determine the number of years it takes for an investment to double in value, you can divide 72 by the annual rate of return. It helped me understand the power of compound interest and starting saving early in life.

The Margin of Safety: This concept involves making investments or financial decisions with a "cushion" of safety, in case things don't go as planned. For example, you may choose to invest in a low-risk portfolio, or only invest a portion of your savings in higher-risk investments.

The Power of Compounding: This model recognizes the power of earning interest on your investments, which in turn earns interest, leading to exponential growth over time.

The Opportunity Cost: This model considers the cost of an opportunity in terms of the benefits foregone by choosing a different option. Businesses usually die of indigestion, not starvation. Indigestion is a failure of carefully considering opportunity costs and building a prioritization framework that takes these tradeoffs.

The 50-30-20 Rule: This rule suggests dividing your after-tax income into three parts: 50% for necessities, 30% for discretionary spending, and 20% for savings and investments. By following this rule, you can prioritize your finances and make the most of your income.

By embracing effective financial planning and leveraging the power of proven frameworks and mental models, we have the ability to transform your circumstances and create a future of abundance and security.

What results you can hope to see:

While we cannot alter the past and the future remains uncertain, actively planning our finances during life's changes significantly improves our present circumstances.

By assuming control over our financial well-being, we have the power to:

Improve your financial security
Have a better handle on your budget
Minimize financial risks
Achieve your financial goals
Stay informed on changes that may impact your finances.

Planning your finances allows us to prepare for the present and any future opportunities that may arise. Over time, the diligent efforts begin to bear fruit. I successfully built my emergency fund, paid off loans, and saved enough for a house and afford a lifestyle where everyday growth is a priority. My financial stability now allows me to weather future changes, such as job transitions and economic fluctuations, with confidence and ease.

#2

Adapting to changes in the economy

On the Outside:

The economy affects every aspect of our lives, from the security of our jobs and how much money we can spend to our ability to borrow money and invest. In my mind, I often envision the economy as the weather, while our finances are like a garden. Just as weather conditions impact the health and growth of plants, changes in the economy significantly influence our financial stability and growth. Understanding this connection empowers us to make informed decisions, adapt to economic fluctuations, and cultivate a thriving financial garden even in the face of uncertainty.

"Predicting rain doesn't count. Building arks does."

- Warren Buffet

When the economy is going through changes, there are several indicators that I have come to observe as common patterns.

Here are a few of them:

High unemployment rates: When the economy is struggling, companies may lay off employees, leading to higher unemployment rates. We have seen this happening during the global financial crisis of 2008 and the more recent COVID-19 pandemic.

Decreased consumer spending: Reduced consumer spending - economic concerns often lead people to curtail their expenses, resulting in a decline in consumer spending, which has a detrimental effect on various sectors of the economy.

Stock market fluctuations: Changes in the economy can cause the stock market to rise or fall, which impacts investments and retirement accounts.

Difficulty getting credit: During a recession or major economic downturns, lenders are more hesitant to lend money, making it harder to get loans or credit.

Business closures - when the economy is weak, many businesses struggle to stay afloat and may ultimately close their doors.

All of these have a ripple effect, impacting not only personal finances but also the overall health of the economy.

On the Inside:

To put this simply, just as a river can be influenced by many different factors such as weather patterns, terrain, and human activities, the economy is also shaped by a complex mix of forces. Changes to any one of these factors can cause ripples or waves that impact the flow of the river or in our case the state of the economy.

"Trying to predict the future of the economy is like trying to shoot a bullet at a flying bird. You might get lucky once, but most of the time you'll miss."

- Peter Lynch

Understanding the causes of economic changes can be intricate and involve multiple factors.

Several common contributors to a changing economy include:

Government policies - Changes in government policies, such as changes to tax laws, trade agreements, or regulations, have a significant impact on the economy.

Business cycles - The economy goes through periods of expansion and contraction, known as business cycles, which is influenced by a variety of factors such as changes in consumer spending, interest rates, and inflation.

Global events - Major global events, such as pandemics, natural disasters, or geopolitical conflicts, also impact the economy.

Technology - Technological advancements disrupt industries and change the way businesses operate, leading to changes in the economy.

Demographics - Changes in population size and demographics have a long-term impact on the economy, influencing things like workforce availability, consumer spending patterns, and government spending priorities.

By understanding and embracing these root causes, we can proactively adjust our strategies, investments, and decision-making to thrive in changing economic conditions.

What Decisions do you need to consider?

Imagine you're on a rollercoaster that suddenly goes off the tracks and starts running down a hill. That is what happens when the economy takes a sudden downturn. You're holding on for life, career, lifestyle, and whatnot wondering when the ride is going to end!

Adapting to changes in the economy feels overwhelming, but with the right tools we can analyze our situations, identify patterns, and make strategic decisions that aligns with our goals.

The mental models I'm about to share have had a significant impact on my own financial journey, helping me navigate economic changes with confidence and empowerment.

Diversification - By not placing all our eggs in a single basket, we avoid the risk of losing everything should that basket fall. Similarly, it's important to diversify our investments across different asset classes and industries to mitigate risks.

Emergency Fund - "Saving for a rainy day": Just like how we save an umbrella for a rainy day, it's important to have an emergency fund set aside to help you weather financial storms. Having 3 - 6 months of funds to sustain is a good start.

Consistency - "Slow and steady wins the race": We all know the tortoise won the race by taking small, consistent steps. Likewise, by consistently making small financial decisions that can have a big impact in the long run. Start early and start small.

Education - Continuous education in personal finance and economic trends is essential. We may not need to be experts, but having knowledge helps us question our decisions, track the economy, and use information to foster growth. By staying informed, we make better choices, adapt confidently, and unlock opportunities for financial success.

Focus on Essential Expenses - During economic uncertainties, prioritize essential expenses and cut back on discretionary spending. This approach helped me maintain financial stability and build an emergency fund for unexpected situations.

Review and Adjust Investments - Assess investment portfolio and consider reallocating assets to align with changing market conditions. Make the effort and consult with a financial advisor to ensure your investment strategy is well-suited to the current economic climate. Don't forget to 'Trust but Verify', it's your money.

There's a popular saying, "Stop and smell the roses," which reminds us to appreciate the little things in life. Similarly, by taking a moment to reflect on our financial situation, acknowledging our accomplishments, and considering actions that align with our goals, we can make wiser decisions for the future and enjoy a more fulfilling financial journey.

What results you can hope to see:

By learning to adapt to changes in the economy, I could achieve financial stability and security, increase my savings, improve my credit score, and grow investments. Additionally, we can make more informed financial decisions and better protect ourselves against financial risks that come along the way.

"The art of life lies in a constant readjustment to our surroundings."

- Kakuzo Okakura

Ultimately, adapting to changes in the economy teaches us to help achieve our financial goals and improve our overall quality of life.

Financial stability and security

Increased savings

Improved credit score

Growing investments

More informed financial decisions

Better protection against financial risks

Achieving financial goals

Improving the overall quality of life.

From the bursting of the Dot Com bubble in the early 2000s to the 2008 Financial crisis and the recent COVID-19 pandemic, the economy has been through many changes. These events highlight how the economy can be impacted. However, by staying aware, anticipating changes, and using the right-thinking models, we can make smart financial decisions that help weather the storm and emerge from economic downturns in a stronger position.

Seek Professional Guidance by consulting with a financial advisor who can provide personalized advice based on your unique financial situation and goals.

#3

Managing Financial Change During Early Parenthood

On the Outside:

Bringing a child into this world can be one of the most blissful and fulfilling experiences of a person's life. It's hard to put into words the pure bliss that comes with cradling your little bundle of joy and witnessing their growth. But let's be honest, how many of us plan for the financial responsibilities that come with early parenthood? It's easy to get lost in the excitement and overlook the reality that having a child is a major financial commitment. From diapers to daycare, the expenses can add up quickly, and before you know it, you may find yourself struggling to manage your finances.

"A *budget is telling your money where to go instead of wondering where it went.*"

\- *Dave Ramsey*

We tend to focus only on the joyous parts of parenthood and forget to plan for the financial responsibilities that come with it.

Here are some of my experiences and observations:

Struggling to manage finances during early parenthood, asking for help from parents;

Increased reliance on loans or credit cards to cover daily expenses or medical bills

Difficulty in paying bills and meeting financial commitments on time

Cutting back on essentials such as food, healthcare, and education to meet expenses related to the child

Difficulty in saving or investing for the child's future or for emergencies

Strained relationships with partners or family members due to financial stress

Delayed or inadequate financial planning for the child's education or marriage

Ignoring the importance of life insurance, health insurance, and other financial products for the family's security and well-being

Difficulty in managing unexpected expenses, such as medical emergencies or home repairs, due to lack of savings or financial planning.

On the Inside:

I never realized how difficult it could be to manage finances during early parenthood. When my wife and I had our first child, we were so focused on the joy and excitement of becoming parents that we didn't give much thought to the financial implications. But then reality set in. The cost of diapers, formula, and baby clothes quickly added up, and we found ourselves cutting back on other expenses just to make ends meet.

And it wasn't just the immediate expenses either. There were also the long-term costs to consider, like saving for our child's education and making sure we had enough money for unexpected expenses. It was overwhelming, to say the least.

"It's not how much money you make, but how much money you keep, how hard it works for you, and how many generations you keep it for."

- Robert Kiyosaki

Here are some key reasons behind financial struggles during early parenthood:

Lack of financial planning and budgeting: Many new parents are unprepared for the expenses that come with having a child and may not have taken the time to create a budget or financial plan to manage these costs. This results in overspending, accumulating debt, and struggling to make ends meet.

Changes in income: A new baby often means taking time off work, reducing hours, or switching to a lower-paying job to accommodate new family responsibilities. This can lead to a decrease in income, making it difficult to meet financial obligations.

Unexpected expenses: From medical bills to unexpected home repairs, unexpected expenses quickly deplete savings and put a strain on finances.

Societal pressures and expectations: Many new parents feel pressure to keep up with the image of the perfect family, which leads to overspending on unnecessary items and activities.

Lack of financial education: Many people are not taught about personal finance in school or at home, which can lead to a lack of knowledge about budgeting, saving, and investing. This makes it difficult to navigate the financial challenges of parenthood.

What Decisions do you need to consider?

During the early stages of parenthood, I faced a tough situation as an entrepreneur. Relocating to a new city and not innovating enough took a toll on our SaaS business, resulting in a decline in client confidence and cashflow. With the arrival of my first child, I had to make a difficult decision for the sake of my family's financial stability. Despite concerns about giving up on my entrepreneurial dreams, I chose to find a job as a Product Manager to secure a consistent income and provide for my growing child. It was a decision driven by love and responsibility, ensuring a secure future for my family.

The experience taught me the importance of staying agile and responsive to family needs and the importance of balancing personal and professional priorities. As a parent, I had to prioritize the needs of my child and make decisions that would ensure our financial stability. It's a lesson that I carry with me to this day and one that has helped me navigate the challenges of parenthood and entrepreneurship.

Here are some practical ideas which worked for me:

Create a budget and stick to it: A budget is a framework for managing our finances and making sure we stay on track with your expenses. It helps us prioritize our spending and identify areas where we can cut back. We can use a spreadsheet or an app to create a budget and track our spending.

The 50/30/20 rule: This is a popular rule of thumb for budgeting. It suggests that 50% of your income should go towards necessities like housing and food, 30% towards discretionary spending, and 20% towards saving and debt repayment or savings.

Emergency fund: It's important to have an emergency fund to cover unexpected expenses like medical bills or car repairs. A good rule of thumb is to save three to six months' worth of living expenses in an easily accessible savings account or liquid fund.

Pay off high-interest debt first: If you have multiple debts, focus on paying off the one with the highest interest rate first. This will save you money in the long run and help you get out of debt faster.

Automate your savings: Set up automatic transfers from your savings account to an investment account. This will make it easier to save money without thinking about it. Scan the QR to find useful resources on how to do it.

Delayed gratification: It's important to distinguish between wants and needs. Delaying gratification on non-essential items helped me save money in the long run.

Increase your income: Look into taking up a side hustle or exploring ways to increase your income within your current job, such as requesting a raise or promotion. If you're Coder, take on side projects. If you're in sales, think about affiliate marketing. If you're a teacher or professor, consider offering tuition classes online/offline. These are just a few examples - regardless of your background, there are numerous opportunities to earn extra income.

I have included free apps and resources that will help you find side gigs and increase your earnings. By staying proactive, adaptable, and focused on our goals, we can create a stable and prosperous foundation for ourselves and our loved ones.

What results you can hope to see:

I keep bringing up examples from one of my favorite games - Jenga! Like a game of Jenga, you carefully remove the unstable pieces of debt and overspending, and try to balance them with the stable pieces of income and savings. If you do it right, you can build a strong and stable financial tower that will benefit your family's quality of life. But if you make the wrong move, it can all come crashing down. With a disciplined approach and smart planning, you can soon be a Jenga master and enjoy the rewards of financial stability.

Once you have learned to manage financial changes during early parenthood, you can reap the following rewards:

Reduced financial stress: By having a clear plan for managing your finances, you can reduce the stress and anxiety that comes with financial uncertainty.

Improved credit score: By reducing debt and making on-time payments, you can improve your credit score, which can lead to better interest rates on loans and credit cards.

Increased savings: By creating a budget and setting aside money for savings, you can build an emergency fund and save for future expenses, such as your child's education or retirement.

Better quality of life: By having more financial stability, you can enjoy a better quality of life with your family, including the ability to take vacations, participate in activities and hobbies, and create lasting memories.

As I look back on my journey, I've come to understand the importance of learning from past experiences, making effective plans, and staying resilient. By consistently reviewing and adjusting our financial strategies as our families grow, we can navigate the challenges and confidently embrace the joys of parenthood while ensuring a strong financial foundation for our loved ones.

#4
Navigating Financial Change in the Digital Age

On the Outside:

The financial landscape is rapidly changing due to technological innovation, with traditional practices being disrupted. Digital platforms, mobile banking, cryptocurrency, and blockchain are revolutionizing how we save, invest, and transact. The financial industry is shifting towards customer-centricity, personalization, and automation, enabling more individuals and businesses to access services that were once out of reach. India's UPI and ONDC are leading global innovations. Navigating financial change in the Digital Age is not easy since it is constantly evolving.

"The future of finance is digital, and those who can adapt will thrive."

- Jamie Dimon

The digital age has revolutionized the financial industry, making it easier for individuals to access financial services and products through digital platforms.

However, this ease of access has also brought about a host of new challenges. Some worth noting include:

Lack of Digital Literacy: The emergence of UPI and other Neo banking platforms in India has accelerated the pace of technological change, challenging traditional banks and cash-based transactions. Today, the need to educate ourselves on digital financial platforms and how to use them safely and effectively is very important.

Over Reliance on Debt: Obtaining loans through options like "early salary," "overdraft," and "buy now, pay later" is easier than ever before. This has led to a rise in financial stress, increased debt burden, and a negative impact on credit scores, which have long-term consequences to financial well-being especially if you are in your 20's & 30's.

Lack of Financial literacy: The digital age has accelerated the discovery of financial products through apps and self-service interfaces, making transactions easier to execute. However, without understanding the underlying concepts of financial instruments, using digital tools alone may not be enough to make money work in your favor.

Data & Personalization: Data is the new oil, but its use for personalized services and products creates a trade-off between convenience and protection of customer rights, with concerns over data privacy, security, and potential bias and discrimination through algorithmic decision-making.

Information overload: With so many financial products and services available through digital channels, it is natural for you to struggle to keep up with the sheer volume of information and make informed decisions.

Cybersecurity threats: As more financial transactions move online, the risk of cyber-attacks and data breaches increases, which can lead to significant financial losses and damage if you are not aware of the threats.

On the Inside:

As much as we'd like to blame the digital age or the financial industry for the evils of financial change, the real villain is often ourselves. Our desire for convenience and quick gratification often leads us to overlook the potential consequences of our financial decisions. We want to access financial services and products quickly and easily, but we don't take the time to understand how they work or the risks involved.

> *"In the digital age, financial literacy is not an option, but a necessity."*
>
> *- Atal Bihari Vajpayee*

We click "I Agree" to terms and conditions without reading them, and we rely on algorithms to make decisions for us without questioning their accuracy or fairness. In a way, we are the architects of our own financial problems. Here are some of the root causes behind the challenges posed by financial change in the digital age.

Lack of Digital Literacy:

Rapid technological advancements

Insufficient education and training on digital financial tools

Limited access to digital platforms and infrastructure

Over Reliance on Debt:

Easy availability of loans through digital channels

Lack of financial planning and budgeting skills

Pressure to keep up with societal expectations and consumption patterns

Lack of Financial Literacy:

Complexity of financial products and instruments

Insufficient education and training on financial concepts

Limited access to financial guidance and advice

Data & Personalization:

Collection and use of vast amounts of data by financial institutions

Lack of regulations and standards to ensure data privacy and security

Potential for bias and discrimination in algorithmic decision-making

Information Overload:

Overwhelming volume of information and options available on digital platforms

Limited capacity to process and analyze information effectively

Difficulty in discerning reliable and trustworthy sources of information

Cybersecurity Threats:

Increasing reliance on digital platforms for financial transactions

Sophistication and prevalence of cyber-attacks and data breaches

Limited awareness and understanding of cybersecurity risks and best practices.

What Decisions do you need to consider?

My Grandmother used to say the art of cooking is all about a mix of ingredients, precision, and a dash of creativity. Similarly navigating financial change in the digital age requires a mix of skills, knowledge and discipline.

To come out winning in the digital age of finance, here's a handful of key decisions and strategies that can be used to overcome the challenges posed by financial change in the digital age.

If you can't grow it, don't lose it: Stick to what you know and understand, just like sticking to a recipe you know by heart. By staying within your "Circle of Competence," you can make informed financial decisions and avoid financial disasters.

Build a Strong Financial Foundation: What's the financial foundation? The basics lie in developing a budget, managing debt effectively, and investing wisely. One mental model that I have used in my 20's is the "10-10-10 Rule," which encourages you to think about the impact of your decision on the next 10 minutes, 10 months, and 10 years. By considering the short-term and long-term consequences of your decisions, you can build a strong financial foundation that will serve you well in the future.

Diversify Investments: Diversifying investments is an important strategy for mitigating risk and maximizing returns. I wish I knew the "Margin of Safety" framework early enough before losing 70% of my investments during the 2008-09 recession. It emphasizes the importance of investing in assets that are undervalued or have a margin of safety. By diversifying investments and seeking out undervalued assets, we can minimize risk and maximize returns.

I am feeling lucky! Cybersecurity is not a paper you study, or feel lucky about. Just like how a bouncer checks IDs to keep a party secure, you can use the "Zero Trust" framework to keep your financial information and assets secure. By layering security measures, you can make it much harder for hackers to break in and access your personal information.

Before you Swipe: Every financial investment instrument comes with fine print, so it's important to take the time to understand the risks and benefits of each investment. Always seek professional advice, but at the same time do your own research. Ultimately, it's your money on the line, not theirs. Digital Fin-tech products intentionally make clicking, swiping, and tapping easy. Buying groceries or a dress is one thing, but purchasing investment products is a completely different matter. Take the time to do your own research and analysis - 'Trust but Verify'.

What results you can hope to see:

The one thing you would certainly see is money working for you 24/7/365 if you navigate your finances in this fast-paced Digital Age. Digital gives you the speed of execution and choice, all you need is the right direction and avoid the common pitfalls.

"Speed without direction is useless"

- Tony Robbins

Here's what success may look like as a result of overcoming the challenges posed by navigating financial change in the digital age:

Increased financial literacy and understanding of financial instruments, leading to better decision-making and potentially higher returns on investments.

Stronger financial foundation built through effective budgeting, debt management, and wise investing, leading to long-term financial stability and security.

Diversified investment portfolio, leading to reduced risk and potentially higher returns.

Understanding of Cybersecurity, leading to protection of personal and financial information and assets from cyber threats.

With increased awareness and understanding of the risks and benefits of financial products in this Digital era, we can make informed decisions and potentially get better investment outcomes. Imagine the year in the future where you no longer work for money, instead money is working for you. By fixing your present, you arm yourself to lead a life where you have the freedom to pursue your passions and live the life you want without worrying about financial stress.

#5

Navigating Financial Change due to Job loss

On the Outside:

In times of change, there are always opportunities and challenges that come with it. During COVID 19 pandemic, I was fortunate enough to have a job, but millions of people lost their livelihoods overnight, some were close friends and loved ones. Witnessing this level of depression and despair can be enough to break even the strongest of individuals.

In the past, I also experienced the pain of losing a job, where customers rejected products that my team and I had put so much passion and effort into building. Shutting down my division and having to let go of employees I had hired with big promises was not an easy task. As a leader, it affects you deeply when you have to let down your team, investors, and the community you promised to serve.

"The only real security that a man can have in this world is a reserve of knowledge, experience, and ability."

- Henry Ford

It was a tough blow when I had to dissolve my team and exit my job due to the closure of the whole division. I was caught off guard, and the external circumstances of the job loss caused chaos in my life, especially since my elder son Divit was only three years old at the time.

Here are some of the challenges I had to face:

Difficulty paying bills and expenses: Without a regular source of income, it was challenging to cover necessary expenses such as home loan EMI, bills, utilities, and groceries. The vicious cycle of late payments, missed payments, or even defaulting on loans starts here.

Cutting back on spending: All our discretionary spending such as dining out, entertainment, and travel were cut down. As a couple it caused feelings of deprivation and isolation.

Seeking financial assistance: When I lost my job, my wife's income and my parents' support helped us meet our basic expenses. However, I saw many people resorting to expensive loans and mortgages to make ends meet. Not earning can put a strain on relationships with family and friends, and it can be challenging to deal with the stigma and shame associated with seeking financial assistance...

Selling assets: Most of my team got new jobs within a couple of months, but for a few long-term unemployment led to selling assets such as bikes, cars, or other possessions to generate income or pay off debt. Some returned to their home town and never came back to the city.

Changes in lifestyle: I had to go through significant changes in lifestyle to manage expenses. But many in my team had to resort to downsizing to a smaller home, relocating to a cheaper area, or taking on additional work to make ends meet.

On the Inside:

No matter how much we want to attribute the blame to external factors such as government, policies, new technology, or management decisions, as employees, we do not have any say over being asked to leave. The severance package may only last for a limited time, especially if you are a junior executive. The event of job loss is not what defines you, but your ability to recover from it and move forward will determine how you navigate and emerge from the situation.

"By failing to prepare, you are preparing to fail."

- Benjamin Franklin

Job loss can be accompanied by various factors that lead to financial change. Based on my personal career experiences.

Here are some of the underlying factors that can come into play:

Economic Factors: A downturn in the economy, a recession, or changes in industry or sector often leads to job losses.

Structural Changes: Technological advancements, automation, and outsourcing lead to changes in the job market, resulting in job losses. This also creates new job roles.

Company Restructuring: Changes in the company's operations, mergers, acquisitions, or reorganizations can result in layoffs or job losses.

Personal Factors: Health issues, family responsibilities, or personal circumstances can lead to job loss.

Poor Performance: Poor performance, disciplinary issues, or conflicts with management can lead to termination of employment.

Business Failure: Losses or failure of a business can result in job losses for its employees.

Natural Disasters: Natural disasters, such as floods, earthquakes, or hurricanes, can lead to job loss if businesses are affected or destroyed.

While certain factors that contribute to job loss may be outside of our control, it's important to recognize that there are also factors within our control. The key factor in navigating such circumstances is being prepared for the worst.

What Decisions do you need to consider?

During my college days in Chennai, I would give missed calls as a way for my family and friends to call me back. It was a part of my identity, and I was content with that. However, as I started earning enough to afford a motorbike and upgrade to a Nokia 6601, I no longer relied on missed calls. I had formed a new identity. Our job or career often becomes an integral part of our identity, and experiencing a sudden loss of that identity can greatly impact our emotional and psychological well-being.

The journey of transformation begins with acknowledging our present state. It took me a long time to overcome denial and truly understand and accept the real reasons why I found myself in a situation of job loss. If you find yourself in a similar position.

Here are some actionable steps to consider based on your current circumstances:

Take care of yourself: I know this is not what you'd like to hear faced with challenges. Make sure to take care of your physical and mental health during this time. This includes getting enough sleep, eating a healthy diet, and finding excuses to keep the body moving. Don't shy away from professional help from a therapist or counselor if you are struggling with depression or anxiety.

Acknowledge and accept your feelings: It is important to acknowledge and accept your feelings. Allow yourself to feel these emotions and express them in a healthy way, such as through talking with a trusted friend or family member or through writing a personal diary. We all are gifted in some way, find your gift, none can or will be able to do it for you except yourself!

Network and seek support: Reach out to your professional and personal network for support and guidance. Networking can also lead to new job opportunities and connections in your desired field. LinkedIn and Fishbowl App are great platforms to ask for help, and more often than not people help spread your message to someone who can help you out.

Utilize your emergency corpus: If you have an emergency corpus, use it to cover your monthly expenses until you find a new job. If you don't have one, review your portfolio to see if you can create one such as combining small balances scattered through many accounts, or even physical gold.

Keep paying EMIs: Even if you have lost your job, don't stop paying your EMIs. Falling behind on payments can lead to hefty penalties and negatively impact your credit score. Don't default on Credit card and loan EMIs.

Don't touch your EPF and PPF: These investments are meant for your retirement and should be avoided as a source of emergency funds during job loss. Withdrawing from them can hurt your long-term financial goals.

Track your spending and budgeting: Have an open discussion with your family about your job loss and agree on a revised budget. Budgeting helps you make the right decisions on where to spend your available money. Keep a check on your spending and limit non-essential expenses during this phase.

Identify your strengths and values: Take some time to reflect on your strengths, values, and interests. This can help you gain a better understanding of yourself and can lead to new career opportunities that align with your passions.

Learn new skills: Park a budget for taking courses or attending workshops to learn new skills and improve your knowledge in a particular area. This can not only make you more employable but can also help boost your confidence & network.

Stay positive and focused: Job loss can be a stressful and difficult experience, but try to stay positive and focused on your goals. Use this time to evaluate your career goals and explore new opportunities.

We have to be ready to encounter such situations in life. Going through a job loss changed my relationship with finance, making me see it in a different light altogether. Remember, navigating financial change due to job loss will be challenging, but with a positive mindset, a plan of action, and the right support, you can overcome this hurdle and come out stronger on the other side.

What results you can hope to see:

Our tendency towards consumerism has led us to buy beyond our means. We often rely on our future income when using credit cards or making purchases with buy-now-pay-later options. On the other hand, I have seen my parents always relied on their past income to make purchases, avoiding the risk of borrowing against future income. When I look back, I see how this simple approach can help in staying within one's budget, and being less impacted by sudden cash flow challenges caused by job loss or other unexpected events.

I live with the thought that today will be the last day of my job. I can be fired / replaced any moment irrespective of my legacy which I created over the years in the company or business. It is the planning of such an event which makes someone prepared in advance and sift through the tough tides.

"What doesn't kill you makes you stronger"

- German philosopher, Friedrich Nietzsche

Congratulations! This is the end of the gloomy tunnel, you have made your way out of it!

And here is what you will see as a result of your hardships that you have been through due to the loss of job:

You have built a stronger financial muscle: By taking proactive steps to manage your finances, you will improve your financial stability and reduce the impact of job loss on your overall financial health.

Increased financial literacy: Learning about financial management and taking steps to improve your financial situation can increase your overall financial literacy and confidence in managing your money.

Improved credit score: By making timely payments and reducing debt, you will improve your credit score, which will have long-term benefits for your financial health.

Diversified income streams: Exploring alternative income streams and taking steps to build multiple income sources will help you become more financially resilient and less dependent on a single job or income source.

Better financial planning: Developing a financial plan will help you set goals and create a roadmap for achieving them. You end up making better financial decisions and ultimately achieve greater financial security and success.

So, keep dreaming, keep pushing forward, and keep believing in yourself. The best is yet to come, and your story is far from over. Embrace the challenges, seize the opportunities, and let your resilience shine through. You are capable of achieving greatness, and the world is waiting for the remarkable contributions you have yet to make.

Ready starters for this Chapter to start implementing:

(Scan this QR for Mental Models, Links to Proven Frameworks and Excel templates to get started)

3

RELATIONSHIPS AND CHANGE

As a young boy, my world revolved around my grandmother because my working parents were only around now and then. This shaped me into a bit of a quiet person. I preferred my own company, yet put me in a dark room, and I suddenly yearned for someone else nearby! However, I've been told that when I'm put into social situations, I transform. I become easy to talk to, funny, and witty. Although I can make friends quickly, I find it hard to continue putting in the effort required to maintain those friendships as time passes. This struggle sometimes affects the trust others place in me, as building trust requires consistent effort and communication over time.

My life took a beautiful turn when I met my wife in school. We've walked life's path together for over 20 years. Our journey blessed us with two wonderful kids, Divit and Joel. My wife, unlike me, is a natural at forming and keeping strong bonds with people from all kinds of backgrounds. Her honest kindness, respect, and humility come straight from the values her parents taught her.

This difference between us really highlights how crucial trust is in any relationship. It's the bridge that connects us, the pathway for open communication, and the framework for shared experiences. We humans have a natural desire to connect with those we respect and trust.

The same principle holds in the professional world. Caring for and nurturing relationships paves the way for growth and bigger opportunities. It's a simple equation - the more people who trust and know you, the more chances you get to expand your business. It doesn't matter if it's business to business(B2B) or business to customer(B2C), in the end, it's all about human to human(H2H) connections. And to keep these connections strong, we need to adapt and be responsive to ever-changing needs and dynamics.

Developing strong relationships requires adapting and responding to evolving needs and dynamics.

I recently came across a fascinating concept by British anthropologist Robin Dunbar called the "Dunbar's number". According to him, our brain can only handle up to 150 social relationships effectively. This number includes five loved ones as the closest circle, followed by 15 good friends, 50 friends, 150 meaningful contacts, 500 acquaintances, and 1500 people we can recognize. As we grow and evolve, our relationships change, and it becomes more important to prioritize depth over breadth when it comes to our connections with others.

In this chapter we explore the importance of vulnerability, adaptability, and balance in managing change and maintaining healthy relationships in different stages and contexts of life.

Some key topics on how changes impact your relationships

#1. The Power of Vulnerability: Embracing Change in Your Relationships

#2. From Solo to Duo: Managing Change in Relationships When Moving in Together

#3. Evolution of Relationships: Adapting to Change Over Time

#4. Balancing Independence and Connection: How to Manage Change in Relationships as You Pursue Your Dreams

#5. Embracing Change in the Digital Age: Managing the Impact of Technology on Relationships

#1
The Power of Vulnerability: Embracing Change in Your Relationships

On the Outside:

In any relationship, vulnerability can be a double-edged sword. While it can lead to deeper connections and stronger bonds, it also requires a certain level of risk-taking. When you open up about your feelings, you are putting yourself in a position to be hurt or rejected. Despite this, vulnerability remains a crucial aspect of building strong relationships. It allows us to create safe spaces where others can be themselves, fostering trust and authenticity.

Here are some examples of what can happen when you are not open about your feelings in different types of relationships in personal and professional life:

Unfulfillment or dissatisfaction in romantic relationships, leading to communication breakdowns, misunderstandings, and unresolved conflicts.

Emotional and physical drift in marriages, escalating conflicts, and disengagement, leading to loneliness and isolation.

Distance and misunderstandings in parent-child relationships, with children feeling pressure to conform and parents being unaware of their child's concerns.

Strained relationships with friends and siblings due to unequal giving, misunderstandings, and superficiality.

Lack of trust and communication in team relationships, leading to inefficiencies, missed opportunities, and potential failure or delays.

Dissatisfied clients due to lack of communication and trust, missed expectations, and inability to adapt to changing needs.

Damaged business partnerships due to conflicts, failed negotiation, and inability to adapt to market changes.

On the Inside:

During my college years in Chennai, I used to conceal the fact that I hailed from a small town from Agartala, in North east India. As a freshman, I was often subjected to bullying and looked down upon by my big city seniors. To avoid being treated differently, I kept my background under wraps and played it safe. But it lasted only a few weeks. Eventually I was exposed and faced the ragging and bashing anyways - there was no escaping it! As I grew older, I realized that hiding my vulnerabilities prevented me from being authentic and forming genuine connections. Whether it's the fear of judgment or rejection, or simply a lack of knowledge about how to handle vulnerability, why are we often hesitant to show our vulnerable side in relationships?

There could be multiple reasons for this behavior. After conducting interviews with various individuals.

Here are some possible explanations:

Fear of rejection: Many people are afraid that if they show vulnerability, their partner may reject them or their relationship may end.

Fear of judgment: Similarly, people may worry that if they show vulnerability, they will be judged or criticized by the other person. This fear can be heightened if the other person is known to be critical or unsupportive.

Societal pressure: Society often portrays vulnerability as a weakness, which can make people feel ashamed or embarrassed to show it.

Past experiences: If someone has been hurt or betrayed in the past, they may have built up emotional walls to protect themselves from future pain.

Self-protection: Some people may feel that showing vulnerability is a sign of weakness or that it makes them too exposed or vulnerable to hurt.

Lack of role models: If someone hasn't seen healthy vulnerability modeled in their family or social circles, they may not know how to do it themselves.

Upbringing: Some people may have grown up in households where emotions were not openly discussed or where vulnerability was discouraged. This can make it difficult for them to express vulnerability later in life.

What Decisions you need to consider:

In India, we grew up hearing the Hindi proverb "daal mein kuch kaala hai" which means "there is something fishy going on". In a trust deficit economy such as in India, lack of trust arises from a variety of factors, including corruption, fraud, and lack of transparency. But Customers, clients, and colleagues are looking for genuine, honest, and transparent interactions, and are more likely to engage with individuals and organizations that are open and authentic. One of the best ways to demonstrate trust is showing your vulnerable side to the world. To do that you need to develop a mindset shift through conscious effort and persistence.

By adopting a 'growth mindset', we can embrace vulnerability as a natural part of the learning and growth process. Instead of seeing vulnerability as a weakness, we see it as a strength that allows us to connect with others on a deeper level and learn from our experiences.

"The best way to find out if you can trust somebody is to trust them."

- Ernest Hemingway

Here are the actions you should consider taking to embrace vulnerability, instill trust and become growth minded:

Reflect on your emotions and be open about them: It's important to be honest about your feelings in your relationships, whether it's with your partner, family, or friends. This helps build trust and strengthens your connection.

Communicate effectively: Make sure to express yourself clearly and listen actively when others share their feelings with you. Practice healthy conflict resolution skills to work through disagreements and challenges.

Manage your expectations: Be realistic about what you expect from your relationships. Understand that change is inevitable and that it's okay to have ups and downs in your relationships.

Prioritize self-care: Taking care of your physical, mental, and emotional health is crucial to building strong relationships. Make time for activities that bring you joy and help you recharge.

Embrace vulnerability: Allow yourself to be vulnerable and take risks in your relationships. This can lead to deeper connections and more meaningful experiences.

I found the "ABCDE" model developed by psychologist Albert Ellis useful to identify and challenge our negative beliefs and replace them with more positive ones, leading to a shift in your mindset. Remember that embracing vulnerability and change can be difficult, but it's worth the effort to build strong and meaningful relationships in your life.

What Results you can hope to see:

By embracing vulnerability and managing change in your relationships, you can expect to see a positive shift in your overall well-being and the quality of your relationships.

Here are some of the potential results you can expect to see:

Greater emotional intimacy: As you become more comfortable with vulnerability, you may find that you can share your thoughts and feelings more openly with your loved ones, leading to a deeper emotional connection.

Improved communication: By practicing open and honest communication, you can avoid misunderstandings and strengthen your relationships.

Increased trust: Being vulnerable can help build trust with others as they see that you are willing to show your true self.

Greater resilience: Learning to manage change in your relationships can make you more resilient, helping you to better navigate challenges in other areas of your life as well.

Increased self-awareness: Being vulnerable and embracing change can help you gain a better understanding of your own emotions and needs, leading to greater self-awareness and personal growth.

In the realm of relationships, embracing vulnerability and embracing change go hand in hand. By courageously opening ourselves up, we invite growth, authenticity, and profound connections into our lives.

#2

From Solo to Duo: Managing Change in Relationships When Moving in Together

On the Outside:

On Sunday mornings, my girlfriend and I would enjoy a delightful meal of bread toasts, rajma gravy, and lemon rice. The towering height of the toast stack would put even Burger King's burgers to shame! We'd also rent movies to watch together and spend quality time beating the Chennai heat with just a ceiling fan, we couldn't afford AC or Cooler. Time would fly, and before we knew it, evening had arrived, and my girlfriend had to return to her hostel before the cut-off time.

As time passed, I moved from Polytechnic to an Engineering college near the city, and our closeness only grew stronger. We didn't like being apart, so we took a bold step in the conservative and traditional city of Chennai. We rented a house and started living together, marking our Solo to Duo moment!

Here are some potential factors that may come into play when transitioning from living solo to living as a duo:

Physical space: Sharing a living space can be a significant adjustment. Each person may have different preferences and habits regarding cleanliness, organization, and decor.

Financial responsibility: When moving in together, it is important to establish financial responsibilities, such as rent, utilities, and groceries. Decisions about who pays for what can cause conflict and tension.

Social circle: Moving in together impacted our social circles. Each partner has different friends and interests, and it can be challenging to find a balance that works for both.

Daily routines: Each person may have different daily routines and schedules, which can impact the relationship. For example, one partner may be an early riser while the other prefers to stay up late.

Personal boundaries: When living together, it is important to establish personal boundaries and respect each other's privacy. This can include things like alone time, personal space, and respecting each other's belongings.

On the Inside:

Living with someone can be a whole new experience that reveals the unfiltered and unvarnished version of the person you are sharing your space with. While dating, people tend to dress up and present their best version, but living together reveals personal hygiene habits, moods, attitudes, and other aspects that you might not have been aware of. This new reality can be both exciting and challenging, but it is an opportunity to develop a deeper understanding and appreciation for your partner.

When moving in together, several internal factors can impact a couple's relationship. Some of them are:

Different expectations: Each person may have different expectations for the living situation, such as cleanliness, chores, and personal space.

Communication breakdown: Moving in together can create a new level of intimacy and closeness, which can also lead to conflicts and misunderstandings if communication breaks down.

Personal habits: Living with someone can bring to light personal habits or quirks that may be irritating or difficult to live with, such as snoring or leaving the toilet seat up.

Financial strain: Sharing expenses and budgeting can be a major source of stress and tension for couples, especially if one person is shouldering more of the financial burden.

Adjustment period: Even if both individuals are excited about moving in together, it can take time to adjust to living in the same space and sharing responsibilities. Deciding who does what and managing daily chores can be a learning curve for both.

Overall, moving in together can be a significant change that requires open communication, compromise, and a willingness to adapt to each other's needs and expectations.

What Decisions you need to consider:

Managing a live-in relationship can be a delicate balance. It's a step towards upgrading and graduating your relationship to the next level, where both partners share responsibilities and navigate daily life together. This period serves as a real test before considering a social marriage without actually going through with it. While it's not uncommon for live-in relationships to end, it's actually a smart and logical way for people to be absolutely sure before tying the knot.

Here are some realization i had from my experience:

Set clear expectations: Have an open and honest conversation with your partner before moving in together. It's like building a house on a strong foundation - the more effort you put into laying the groundwork, the more stable the structure will be.

Establish boundaries: Discuss your individual needs and preferences, such as alone time, and work together to find a compromise that works for both of you. It's like setting up a garden with different plants - they each need their own space and care to thrive, but together they can create a beautiful and harmonious space.

Divide household responsibilities: Create a plan for sharing chores and responsibilities to prevent misunderstandings and resentment.

Communicate regularly: Make time to check in with each other and discuss any issues or concerns that arise. It's like maintaining a car - regular check-ups and tune-ups can prevent bigger problems down the road.

Practice empathy: Put yourself in your partner's shoes and try to understand their perspective. It's like seeing the world through different lenses - by understanding and respecting each other's viewpoints, you can find common ground and strengthen your relationship.

Be patient and flexible: Remember that change takes time and be willing to adapt as you navigate this new phase of your relationship. It's like learning a new dance - it may be awkward at first, but with practice and patience, you can find a rhythm and move in sync.

Seek outside help if needed: In urban cities we have access to couples therapy or counseling if you're struggling to adjust to living together. An outside perspective and guidance can make a big difference.

What Results you can hope to see:

Moving in together can be both an exciting and challenging experience. I still remember the first place my girlfriend and I rented - it was a single bedroom house. Back then, I was embarrassed to admit to my friends that we were living together. If someone dropped by without notice, I used to lock my girlfriend inside the bedroom. Looking back, I realize that this was not the right way.

This principle holds true not only for live-in relationships or marriages, but also for business partnerships or collaborations. The dynamics of operating alone versus partnering with someone are vastly different, whether in your personal life or professional endeavors. Working together as a team requires open communication, mutual respect, and a willingness to compromise and adapt.

The living room of the very same house eventually transformed into the office space for our startup, where a team of four diligently worked with minimal resources to secure our first significant client. There was division of space and compromise of privacy, it required adjusting and prioritizing what was most important. Ultimately, compromising on a few things for the greater common goal makes it all worthwhile.

Here are some potential results that can be seen as a result of successfully managing change in relationships when moving in together:

Improved communication: Living together requires open and honest communication, which can lead to better understanding and stronger relationships.

Increased intimacy: Sharing a living space can bring couples closer together and lead to a deeper emotional connection.

Shared experiences: Living together allows couples to share more experiences and create new memories together.

Improved problem-solving skills: Managing a household together can help couples develop stronger problem-solving skills and a greater sense of teamwork.

Increased independence: Living together can help couples become more independent while still maintaining a strong and healthy relationship.

Stronger partnerships: Businesses rely on partnerships and collaborations to grow and expand. By being open to change and working collaboratively with partners, we can build stronger and more successful partnerships.

Greater resilience: Startups face many challenges and setbacks on the path to success. By embracing change and being adaptable, startups can build resilience and stay nimble in the face of adversity.

In summary, whether you are moving in with your significant other or embarking on a new business venture with your team, it all boils down to collaboration. Change is an inevitable aspect of life, and while it can be difficult, with open communication, trust, and a willingness to adapt, you can navigate the changes and emerge stronger on the other side. It's crucial to embrace vulnerability and make thoughtful decisions that align with your values and goals. By doing so, you can create a solid foundation for a long and healthy relationship, both personally and professionally. So, stay open to change, and take the leap with courage and conviction.

#3
Evolution of Relationships: Adapting to Change Over Time

On the Outside:

Our relationships are intricate and have multiple layers. At the core lies the relationship we have with ourselves, followed by our parents who brought us into this world. Then, there's an outer circle that includes extended family, friends, and acquaintances. According to Dunbar's Number, our cognitive capacity allows us to maintain stable social relationships with around 150 individuals. As we grow and change, people enter and exit our social circles. Sometimes circumstances beyond our control push us away from loved ones, while other times we consciously choose to create distance.

Here are some of the challenges my loved ones faced as I went through phases of personal growth and struggled to adapt in my relationships:

Spending less time together: As relationships evolve, my priorities and interests changed, leading to less time spent together with family and friends.

Fighting more often: As I was busy in my personal transformation for change and growth in my startup, my perspectives and opinions on common life matters also changed. This led to more disagreements and conflicts with family and colleagues.

Feeling distant or disconnected: When you are working on yourself in isolation, your core family and friends may feel less connected and distant from you. This can be due to a variety of factors, including changes in work, hobbies, or other life circumstances.

Changing social circles: You need to develop new friendships and form new social circles for your work that may not include your partner. This can lead to feelings of isolation or loneliness within the relationship.

Changes in intimacy: As we age and experience different life events, our needs and desires around intimacy also change. This sometimes led to conflicts or misunderstandings within a relationship.

On the Inside:

After matriculation when I moved out from my Grandma's place at Agartala to Chennai to attend Polytechnic, I made a conscious decision to let go of my school friends. While a few joined me on the journey, most of them continued their higher secondary education. Saying goodbye was easier said than done.

Back then, incoming mobile phone calls were expensive and we relied on the landline phone of our landlord to receive weekly calls from parents. My girlfriend and I communicated through letters that were delivered by postman. It may seem like a lifetime ago, but it was only the year 2001. Looking back after two decades, I realize that many of my close friends and family members are no longer in my inner circle.

During college, I felt distant from my parents, but since they became grandparents, we have become much closer thanks to the kids. Relationships are constantly evolving, and whether we realize it or not, embrace and appreciate the relationships you have, while also being open to new ones.

Here are some of the underlying causes I found why relationships evolve:

Growing apart: As you change over time, sometimes this causes couples or friends to drift apart. Internal experiences may include feeling less connected or less interested in spending time together.

Different life stages: When you are in different life stages (e.g., one is focused on building a career, while the other is focused on starting a family), this creates tension in a relationship. Internal experiences include feeling misunderstood or unsupported by the other person.

Differing values: As we mature, our values shift or become more pronounced. If two people in a relationship have very different values, it creates conflict. Internal experiences may include feeling frustrated or resentful.

Past baggage: Everyone has emotional baggage, but it can become more pronounced as you get older. Past traumas or experiences impact the way people relate to each other in a relationship. Internal experiences may include feeling triggered or defensive.

Loss or grief: Experiencing a loss or going through a period of grief also impacts relationships. Internal experiences include feeling isolated or unsupported.

Communication breakdown: Your inability to express your feelings or ideas openly with your partner leads to misunderstandings and a breakdown of intimacy.

Trust issues: Trust is a foundation of any relationship, and when it is broken, it is very difficult to regain. This can be due to infidelity, dishonesty, or a breach of confidentiality.

Fear of change: As you and your partner grow and change, you may experience fear and uncertainty about the future of your relationship. This leads to resistance to change or a lack of motivation to work on the relationship.

Unrealistic expectations: Unrealistic expectations, whether they be about your partner or the relationship itself, can lead to disappointment and resentment over time.

What Decisions you need to consider:

In life, change is inevitable, especially in relationships. Like a caterpillar transforming into a butterfly, relationships also evolve and change over time. It's important to embrace this natural progression and adjust accordingly. Just like a butterfly needs to spread its wings to fly, we too need to be open and communicate honestly with our loved ones to navigate changes. By compromising and negotiating, we can adapt to the changes and find opportunities for growth. Remember to focus on the positive aspects of change, stay connected with your support system, and visualize a positive outcome. Like a butterfly emerging from its cocoon, we too can emerge from relationship changes stronger and more resilient.

Here are some helpful tips to guide you through the process:

Practice self-reflection to gain a better understanding of your needs and desires in the relationship. This can help you communicate more effectively and make decisions that align with your values. I will attribute this as the topmost tip of all.

Communicate openly and honestly with your partner/friend/family member about your feelings, needs, and concerns. This can help you both navigate changes and strengthen your relationship.

Be willing to compromise and negotiate when needed. Changes in relationships often require flexibility and willingness to adjust expectations and habits.

Focus on the positive aspects of the change and look for opportunities to grow and learn. This helps us stay optimistic and open-minded.

Stay connected with your social support network, including friends, family, and community groups. Having a strong support system helps us manage stress and feel more secure during times of change.

Use visualization techniques to help us picture a positive outcome and feel more confident in our ability to adapt to change. Imagine yourself successfully navigating the change and experiencing positive growth in your relationship.

Remember, change can be challenging, but it can also lead to positive growth and development in our relationships. With the right mindset and strategies, we can adapt to changes and continue to build strong, healthy relationships.

What Results you can hope to see:

I am deliberate in filling up the spots in my top 3 Dunbar circles. I prefer staying away from those who sap my energy, blame others for their problems, or spread toxic gossip. Raising kids can be energy draining too, and answering a seven-year-old's "why" questions demands patience like no other! But family and close ones require our support, and we can't avoid our responsibilities, no matter how overwhelming they feel. They are your closest Durbar circle, followed by your best friends and good friends.

Some people find contentment in having a few close relationships, while others seek a larger social network in today's Instagram age. Nonetheless, the quality of the connections and the support they offer is more vital than the quantity.

Here are some potential outcomes that you can aspire to observe as a result of adapting to changes over time in your relationships:

Improved communication: By being adaptable and open to change, you will find that your communication with your partner or loved ones becomes more honest and productive.

Increased intimacy: As you and your partner adapt to changing circumstances and grow together, you will find that your intimacy and connection deepens.

Greater emotional resilience: Adapting to change can be challenging, but it can also help you develop greater emotional resilience and coping skills.

More fulfilling relationships: By being open to change and growth, you will find that your relationships become more fulfilling and rewarding as you evolve.

Greater personal growth: As you navigate changes in your relationships, you will also experience personal growth and development, learning more about yourself and your own needs in the process.

A relationship is not a destination that you reach, but rather a journey that continues to evolve even after marriage, childbirth, or starting a career or business. By consistently putting effort into your relationships and adapting to changes as you grow, they can become a source of strength and support. They provide a solid foundation to lean on during tough times, inspire you to be your best self, and help you stay focused on your goals. By fostering an atmosphere of mutual support and care, we can overcome any obstacle that life may throw our way. Because life will; it always had and always will.

#4
Balancing Independence and Connection: How to Manage Change in Relationships as You Pursue Your Dreams

On the Outside:

I still have an unfulfilled dream, the dream of building and creating an App which will be used daily, repeatedly and finds its place in the home screen of its 10 Million users. I could reach only 10% of that goal with over 2 decades of grunt work based on the opportunities I got and created for myself. I aspire to build, create and impact lives on a mega scale. This gives me a high.

My wife, on the other end, likes to be in the present moment without thinking too much about the future. Being present without much thinking of the future is a wonderful gift to have. It helps you see things as they are and not make up imaginative outcomes and endings in the future.

When we started living together, everything went for a toss. Her office timings don't match mine, sleep cycles were different, choosing what to eat and buy from the supermarket was different. We couldn't relate to what the other was trying to say. Her stories were about corporate politics, new boss's behavior, emotional meltdowns and my stories were about this new tech, sudden breakthrough in product development or insecurities about how to pay salaries next month if we don't generate enough income.

We are not converging on common topics, there were too many divergent topics of discussions and nothing seemed to work out. The only good news was we allowed each other to hear the other out, so we vented out as much as we could!

When pursuing a dream job or startup, there will be many divergent factors which will impact the dynamics of a relationship. They include:

Lack of Time: Working 14+ hours a day for my startup left little room for work-life balance, causing personal aspirations to suffer, and spending quality time with my partner became more of a coincidence than a regular occurrence.

Financial pressure: Pursuing personal dreams comes with financial obligations that may put pressure on our relationship. There were many occasions where I took out my wife's salary to pay salaries to employees during starting up.

Lack of support: Sometimes, pursuing personal goals makes you feel isolated and unsupported in your relationship. Are you surrounding yourself with people who believe in you and your aspirations?

Jealousy: Pursuing personal goals may trigger feelings of jealousy in your partner, especially if you are in the same profession. Are you communicating openly and honestly about your aspirations and how they align with your relationship goals?

Different priorities: Pursuing personal goals may mean that you and your partner have different priorities. Are there any converging topics of interest and a balance that works for both of you?

On the Inside:

When we are busy chasing our goals, we often overlook the warning signs that our relationship may be suffering. We become so engrossed in our daily tasks and responsibilities that we forget to nurture our connection with our partner. This is especially challenging in a bustling city where we may share a roof, but live separate lives. The uncertainty of when we will see each other again can exacerbate the situation.

The underlying causes of this phenomenon may include:

Stress: Pursuing a startup is stressful, especially if you are a 1st generation entrepreneur. And that stress can spill over into personal relationships with your partner. The pressure to succeed creates tension and anxiety that can be difficult to manage.

Time management: Starting a business or pursuing a dream job require a significant amount of time and energy early on. Balancing work and personal life were very challenging, since we had different career goals.

Financial strain: Starting a business will take time to see a return on investment, and the uncertainty of income was very stressful for both of us. As young couples, it was a tough choice to sacrifice lifestyle expenses and act maturely to build your startup.

Differing Beliefs: Pursuing a dream job or startup is also the period where you have maximum personal growth and development. This leads to changes in values, beliefs, and priorities, which impacts personal relationships and the equation of couples.

Decision-making: In pursuing personal goals, we had to make choices that impacted our relationships, such as investing more time in work or sacrificing leisure time. These decisions can lead to tension and conflict in the relationship and unfulfilled desires.

Overall, pursuing a dream job or startup is exciting but a challenging time that requires careful attention to personal relationships. Communication, empathy, and understanding are key to managing change in relationships during this time.

What Decisions you need to consider:

One of the keys to our successful relationship was our willingness to listen to each other. Perhaps this was because our relationship evolved from being school friends to lovers and then spouses. Sharing our personal struggles with each other allowed us to feel a sense of relief. My wife's job and my startup were our respective challenges. By engaging in dialogue, we developed empathy and mutual respect. As a result, we started supporting each other in small ways to help get through the day.

If you are pursuing your dream job or startup, while also maintaining a relationship, it can be challenging to find the right balance between independence and connection.

Here are some decisions to consider:

Communication: Be open and honest with your partner about your goals, aspirations, and the time and energy you need to dedicate to your job or business.

Priorities: Determine your priorities and make sure your partner understands where they stand on your list. Discuss how you can support each other in achieving your goals while maintaining your relationship.

Boundaries: Set boundaries to ensure that your work or business doesn't completely take over your life. Schedule specific times for work and time with your partner.

Support system: Build a support system outside of your relationship, such as friends or mentors who can offer guidance and help you manage the stresses of pursuing your dream job or business.

Flexibility: Be flexible and adaptable when it comes to balancing work and your relationship. Recognize that both require time, effort, and attention, and adjust your approach as needed.

Self-care: Take care of yourself physically and emotionally. Make time for activities that bring you joy and relaxation, and be mindful of your own needs and boundaries.

Shared vision: Discuss your long-term goals as a couple and ensure that they align with your individual aspirations. Having a shared vision can help you navigate the challenges of pursuing your dreams while maintaining a strong relationship.

What Results you can hope to see:

By staying adaptable and flexible, we ensure that our relationships continue to provide us with the support and strength we need to achieve our dreams. We must learn to prioritize our personal aspirations while also recognizing the importance of maintaining strong relationships. It's not an easy task, but with patience, empathy, and a willingness to compromise, we can achieve success in both our personal and professional lives while still nurturing the relationships that matter most.

Here are some potential results you can hope to see when balancing independence and connection in relationships as you pursue your dream job or startup:

Improved communication: When you are transparent and honest about your goals and aspirations, it improves the communication in your relationships. It also led to better support from your loved ones as they understand your priorities.

Increased personal growth: Pursuing your dreams can lead to personal growth and development, which enhances your overall well-being and sense of fulfillment.

Stronger relationships: Balancing independence and connection helps to build stronger relationships based on mutual respect and support.

Greater success: Pursuing your dreams with the support of your loved ones can lead to greater success and achievement in your personal and professional life.

More meaningful connections: By balancing independence and connection, we can cultivate more meaningful and authentic relationships with the people in our life.

I have come to realize that being in a relationship is not just about me and my personal goals, but about us and our collective aspirations. It's about sharing the ups and downs, supporting each other through struggles, and celebrating the wins together. By making each other's goals our own, we can create a shared legacy that we can look back on with pride and inspiration. This journey has taught me that true happiness comes not just from achieving my own individual goals, but from doing so in the context of a loving and supportive relationship.

Ultimately, finding a balance between independence and connection in relationships as you pursue your dream job or startup leads to personal growth, stronger relationships, and greater success.

#5
Embracing Change in the Digital Age: Managing the Impact of Technology on Relationships

On the Outside:

Technology is constantly changing and has its benefits and drawbacks. The pandemic accelerated the pace of change and forced us to adapt quickly. I remember using pagers in college back in 2001, which was a cool way to communicate compared to traditional inland letters and postcards. The launch of Reliance CDMA phones during 2002-03 with free incoming calls was a defining moment in India. The more recent Jio 4G launch revolutionized communication in India in 2016. Video calls have become popular during the pandemic, and even those who were initially hesitant to use them have adapted. For younger generations, video is a more natural form of expression and communication.

But with all this I've personally noticed that I'm spending more time communicating with my friends online than in person, and it feels like we're drifting apart. It's easy to get hooked on technology, and I'm guilty of constantly checking my phone and getting lost in the digital world. Even though social media can create a feeling of connection, I've also felt distanced from my loved ones. The overuse of technology has caused misunderstandings and communication breakdowns, which has led to tension and frustration in my relationships.

In today's digital age, technology has become an integral part of our lives, and it has significantly impacted our relationships.

Here are some signals and observations that you frequently observe as a result of technology's impact on our relationships.

> **Decreased face-to-face interaction**: With the rise of social media and messaging apps, people are spending more time communicating online than in person, which leads to a decrease in face-to-face interaction. The pandemic accelerated this even more.

Addiction to technology: People are becoming increasingly addicted to their phones, computers, and other gadgets, leading to a disconnection from the real world and the people around them.

Social isolation: While social media can provide a sense of connection, it also leads to social isolation as people spend more time interacting online than with real-life friends and family.

Communication breakdowns: Misunderstandings and miscommunications arise from the overuse of technology, leading to relationship breakdowns. Communication appears differently depending on whether it's in-person or over the phone.

FOMO (Fear of Missing Out): Social media creates a sense of pressure to constantly be connected and up-to-date on what others are doing, leading to anxiety and stress.

Cyberbullying: Technology has also enabled cyberbullying, which has a severe impact on mental health and relationships.

The impact of technology on our relationships is a double-edged sword. While it has made communication faster and more convenient, it has also led to social isolation, addiction, and communication breakdowns. Overall, while technology brings people closer together, it also leads to negative impacts on relationships if not managed properly.

On the Inside:

As someone who is involved in the shaping and creating technology products, I am aware that a lot of thought and research goes into making products addictive. Immersive technologies are becoming more of a reality, Metaverse is already here. It's fascinating how the psychology behind user behavior is leveraged to make products that customers can't help but love. One book that has truly inspired me is "Inspired: How to Create Tech Products Customers Love" by Marty Cagan. It provides valuable insights on how to create technology products that customers truly enjoy using.

The impact of technology on our relationships is a complex issue with various underlying causes.

Internally, there are several factors how technology affects our relationships:

Trust issues: With the constant availability of technology, it can be tempting to check up on your partner or friends, leading to trust issues and a lack of privacy.

Miscommunication: The use of technology can create miscommunications or misunderstandings, as tone and intent can be difficult to convey online.

Disconnection: While technology can provide a sense of connection, it can also lead to disconnection if it is overused or relied upon too heavily.

Pressure to present a perfect image: Social media can create a pressure to present a perfect image, leading to feelings of inadequacy or anxiety.

Addiction: The constant availability of technology can lead to addiction, which can impact mental health and relationships.

What Decisions you need to consider:

In today's digital age, technology is an integral part of our daily lives, and it has significantly impacted the way we communicate and maintain relationships. The history is a testament to the fact that resisting new technology can lead to stagnation, while adopting and adapting to it can open up new opportunities and possibilities.

Technology has revolutionized the way we communicate, making it easier than ever to stay connected with loved ones, even those living far away. I remember the days when I had to use phone booths to make international calls, but now with apps like WhatsApp, calling is practically free and can be done as many times as desired. However, it has also led to a sensory overload where we are constantly bombarded with notifications, leading to addiction and a disconnection from the real-world human connections.

Here are some strategies that have worked wonderfully well for me over the years to balance technology and its effect on relationships:

Setting boundaries: It's important to set boundaries around technology use, such as limiting screen time or establishing device-free zones such as bedrooms.

Practice mindfulness: Just like how you can be intentional about drinking 8 glasses of water a day to improve your physical health. Adopt a mindful approach to technology use by setting intentions and avoiding mindless scrolling or checking notifications.

Prioritize face-to-face interaction: Prioritize face-to-face interactions with your friends and family and give them more importance than online interactions. You can use special occasions such as birthday parties, wedding celebrations, religious and cultural events as opportunities to meet and catch up with many people in a shorter period of time.

Maintain open communication: It's important to have open and honest conversations with your partner or friends about how technology is impacting your relationship. Particularly in long-distance relationships where a 10-minute video call may not convey the full picture of what you are going through in your day.

Take breaks: Make a conscious effort to take breaks from technology and spend time engaging in other activities. Enjoy the seasons and outdoors. There is no substitute for a hill trek, a walk by the sea, or cozying up at night to watch the stars together.

Don't hesitate to seek help: In India, there's a common belief that only those who are mentally ill need to visit a psychiatrist. However, mental health is as important as physical health, and seeking professional help is essential if technology addiction or cyberbullying is affecting your mental health or relationships. Remember, seeking help is a sign of strength, not weakness.

What Results you can hope to see:

To be honest, finding the balance between technology and relationships can feel like walking on a tightrope. I am still learning how to strike the right balance in my own life. However, the small changes that I have made have resulted in an open and honest relationship with my life partner, business stakeholders, friends, and family in general.

Some of the visible benefits include:

Improved communication: By setting boundaries and prioritizing face-to-face interactions, communication in relationships improved.

Increased trust: Establishing mutual trust and respecting privacy led to deeper trust, which is essential for building successful relationships, both personal and professional.

Stronger relationships: By practicing mindfulness and open communication, relationships have strengthened and deepened.

Improved mental health: Reducing addiction and cyberbullying resulted from technology led to improved mental health and better focus for personal growth.

More fulfilling life: By taking breaks from technology and engaging in other activities, life can become more fulfilling and enjoyable.

In today's rapidly evolving digital world, it's crucial to strike a balance between online interactions and in-person connections. This allows us to nurture authentic intimacy, sustain meaningful relationships, and harness the potential of technology to enhance our lives, while still prioritizing genuine human connections and adapting to the changing landscape.

Ready starters for this Chapter to start implementing:

(Scan this QR for Mental Models, Links to Proven Frameworks and Excel templates to get started)

4

PHYSICAL AND CHANGE

I visited a popular urban park near my place at Newtown, Kolkata with my family for a day's excursion. I was amazed at the diversity of people around me. Young children run and play with joyful abandon, while couples walk hand in hand, enjoying the fresh air and each other's company. Joggers and cyclists speed by, yet as different as they all may seem, there is one thing they all have in common: their physical presence tells a story about their mental state.

Our physical selves often hold clues to our emotional and psychological well-being. A slumped posture may indicate feelings of depression or low self-esteem, while clenched fists and a tense jaw may suggest anxiety or anger. Conversely, a relaxed gait and an open, engaged posture can signal a sense of confidence and inner peace.

It's easy to get caught up in the hustle and bustle of daily life and overlook the signals our bodies are sending us. We may push through fatigue and pain, ignore tension and discomfort, or even numb ourselves with substances in an attempt to avoid difficult emotions. But when we take the time to really look at our physical selves, we can gain valuable insights into our physical, mental and emotional states.

I didn't pay attention to my body's signals for long, especially during college days in Chennai. Whatever, whenever and from where so ever I used to stuff food inside my mouth, without any idea how it will metabolize and digest. In Software Development, we have a saying "Garbage in, garbage out". And that is exactly what was true for me. I was putting in a lot of garbage, and that was affecting my weight, mood and overall well being .

Our bodies, shaped by several years of evolution, are sophisticated machines. By paying attention to the signals our bodies send us, we can identify the underlying causes of health issues, find balance, build resilience, and improve our overall sense of well-being. So, the next time you feel stressed, anxious, or overwhelmed, take a moment to check in with your physical self. Your body is always sending you messages, and you might be surprised by what you learn.

Some key topics on how changes impact your physical being

#1. How Weight Affects Your Health and Well-being

#2. Living with Chronic Illness: Adapting to Physical Changes and Limitations

#3. Technology and Your Physical Health: How Screen Time Affects Your Body

#4. Changing Sleep Patterns: How it Impacts Your Physical Health

#5. Aging Gracefully: Navigating Physical Change as You Grow Older

#1
How Weight Affects Your Health and Well-being

On the Outside:

Being overweight or underweight both can invite judgment and discrimination, perpetuated by the media's portrayal of "perfect" body types. This is especially true in customer-facing or show professions where physical appearance is often prioritized. However, the more pressing concern with weight changes is the impact it has on our physical health.

As someone who is diagnosed with a metabolic disorder, I know firsthand the health challenges that can arise from being overweight. Doctors have informed me that my condition will affect my health for a long time. It's not just a matter of body image or social stigma - being overweight increases the risk of chronic diseases such as diabetes, heart disease, and stroke. Similarly, being underweight can also lead to a range of health problems, including weakened immune function, malnutrition, and a higher risk of osteoporosis.

Weight fluctuations result in a range of external problems that impact how others view and interact with us.

Some examples of external problems of weight fluctuations include:

> **Self-esteem and body image**: Weight fluctuations for me always were on the upper side. It affected my self-esteem and body image, leading to negative emotions and feelings of shame or inadequacy specially in social functions and parties.
>
> **Health challenges**: It's common knowledge that increase in weight impacts overall physical health and increases the risk of chronic health conditions, such as diabetes, heart disease, and certain types of cancer. It is such a low feeling to have when your mind wants to do great things but your body gives up!
>
> **Social stigma**: Whether in school, college or office the society often associates being overweight with negative stereotypes, such as laziness, lack of self-control, and poor health habits. My wife was underweight for

a long time of her life, and she was called "featherweight" during school days. The social stigma and discrimination impact emotional well-being and social interactions.

Clothing challenges: Changes in weight leads to challenges in finding clothing that fits properly. I am guilty of buying clothes from the Kids section for my wife! With changing times, thanks to the awareness and acceptance, many new brands have Plus size clothing options.

Workplace challenges: It's unfortunate to see how your external appearance can often overshadow your skills and abilities in the workplace. I have seen being overweight or underweight have led to unfair judgments from coworkers and bosses, impacting job performance, opportunities for advancement, and overall job satisfaction.

Physical discomfort: If you are not in the right BMI range, it causes physical discomfort, such as joint pain, back pain, and difficulty with mobility. For the ambitious and high achieving aspirants, this becomes a blocker in their path to glory.

Our physical health is closely tied to our weight. Changes in weight, whether overweight or underweight, can have significant impacts on our physical health. Our physical being paves the way for our emotional and psychological well-being.

On the Inside:

Divit was five years old, on a Sunday I weighed him and he was 16 kgs, that was exactly by how much I was overweight! It hit me very hard that I was carrying the same weight as my son, 24x7x365 days. This realization changed everything for me.

From my personal experience, I understood the importance of taking control of my physical health, especially when it comes to weight gain and related health problems. I have learned that poor diet, lack of physical activity, genetics, hormonal imbalances, medications, stress, sleep deprivation, and underlying medical conditions all contribute to weight gain and its related health issues.

Unfortunately, despite the knowledge that over 50% of these underlying causes are within our control, many of us still fail to make the necessary changes to improve our health. I have been guilty of choosing convenience over my health, taking my two-wheeler or car even for the shortest distances, and it has made me less active.

Here are some of the underlying reasons why weight changes impact our physical health:

Poor diet: A diet that is high in calories (read sugar), saturated fats, and processed foods will contribute to weight gain and related health problems. I was addicted to it for a long time, in fact studies suggest sugar is more addictive than cocaine!

Lack of physical activity: Convenience is added into every walk of our lives especially in urban context. A sedentary lifestyle contributes to weight gain and associated health issues. It is known to all of us but most neglected.

Genetics: Genetics contribute to weight gain and related health issues. A family history of obesity suggests a possible genetic predisposition to weight gain.

Hormonal imbalances: Hormonal changes or imbalances, such as those experienced during pregnancy or menopause, contribute to weight gain. I've personally witnessed this with my wife during both of her pregnancies.

Medications: Certain medications contribute to weight gain as a side effect especially allopathic medicine. This is because they affect our metabolism, appetite, and greatly influence how the body stores fat.

Stress: Stress leads to overeating or poor dietary choices, which contribute to weight gain. Overeating gives us a numbing effect and relaxes us in that moment, but creates an addictive vicious cycle which becomes tougher by the day to get out from.

Sleep deprivation: Lack of sleep contributes to weight gain and related health problems. My younger son is currently 1 year old, and my family and I are experiencing severe sleep deprivation. This issue can also arise due to work schedules, such as working with clients in different time zones.

Underlying medical conditions: Certain medical conditions, including thyroid disorders or polycystic ovary syndrome (PCOS), contribute to weight gain and related health problems. I have experienced this with my wife who was diagnosed with a thyroid disorder after pregnancy. Also, my mother couldn't recover post-surgery of thyroid tumor that affected her hormone levels and overall physical health.

These internal problems impact your overall physical and emotional health, making it important to prioritize self-care and seek support when needed. It's important to consult with a healthcare professional to determine the underlying cause of weight changes and develop a personalized plan for managing weight and maintaining physical and emotional health.

What Decisions do you need to consider?

The human body is a complex and sophisticated machine. However, when we are not in the healthy weight range, we put unnecessary stress on the body, which leads to a breakdown of its essential reserves. It's important to understand that our bodies are designed to live in the moment, working optimally when we take care of them through proper nutrition, exercise, and rest.

Here are some decisions I considered to manage weight and improve physical health:

Consult with a healthcare professional: It is important to consult with a healthcare professional, such as a doctor or registered dietitian, to determine the underlying cause of overweight or underweight and develop a personalized plan for managing weight and maintaining physical and emotional health.

What worked for my ancestors, will work for me: As each region has its own seasons, weather, crops, and climate, the diet that suits one region may not work for another. I have found a sustainable and effective way to nourish my body and mind by looking to the wisdom of the past.

Rather than following "foreign" diet plans, I adapted my eating habits based on my ancestral diet while incorporating modern techniques and it worked wonderfully well.

Develop a healthy diet and exercise plan: Developing a healthy diet and exercise plan help us manage weight and improve overall physical health. Consulting with a registered dietitian and a fitness professional help develop a personalized plan based on your needs and goals. More than the plan itself, tracking the progress of the plan is more important.

Seek support: It's important to seek support from friends, family members, or a professional counselor to address emotional challenges related to weight, such as low self-esteem, anxiety, or depression. Find an accountability partner to help each other.

Manage stress: Stress contributes to mood, weight and impacts overall physical and emotional health. Developing stress management strategies, such as practicing mindfulness, yoga, or meditation, helps us manage stress and maintain our emotional well-being. Stress is a natural consequence of growth and progress, and the key is to learn to manage it rather than avoiding or ignoring it.

Prioritize self-care: Make self-care a priority by focusing on activities that enhance our physical and emotional well-being. Start with the basics - sleep, staying hydrated, and engaging in activities that bring you joy and fulfillment. By taking care of ourselves, we become better equipped to support others instead of being a burden to our family.

Seek medical treatment for underlying conditions: Your weight is a good reflector of underlying medical conditions, such as thyroid disorders or hormonal imbalances. The sooner you start medical treatment for underlying conditions the faster you can manage your weight and improve overall health.

In a world of one-click food options at our fingertips, it's common to develop a habit of overeating without purpose. Growing up, I was taught to eat every 3-4 hrs. and avoid an empty stomach. Much later in my life, I have discovered the power of fasting and mindful eating. By adopting a practice of eating until 80% full and incorporating regular fasting daily, weekly, yearly into my routine, I have regained control over my eating habits and experienced a profound sense of empowerment. By making proactive choices and prioritizing our physical and emotional well-being, we can effectively manage weight and lead a fulfilling and healthy life.

What Results you can hope to see:

We are all energy beings in this universe. Self-care pays off. By prioritizing our physical health and well-being, we'll experience a boost in energy, confidence, and overall positivity. The journey of addressing weight and embracing healthy habits result in a range of positive outcomes for our body, mind, and spirit.

I have experienced the below:

Improved physical health: By managing weight and maintaining a healthy lifestyle, we improve our physical health and reduce the risk of chronic health conditions, such as diabetes, heart disease, and certain types of cancer. I was able to shed off 10+ kgs and improve my health to the point where I no longer needed medication for my condition.

Increased self-esteem and body image: Addressing emotional challenges related to weight improved my self-esteem and body image, leading to greater confidence and overall mental health. I no longer looked for outside validation of my body image.

Better relationships: Improving emotional challenges related to weight has helped me build healthy relationships and be more present when around people. I have also learned to appreciate and receive appreciation, resulting in better connections with others.

Increased energy and stamina: By engaging in regular physical activity and maintaining a healthy weight, I could increase my energy and stamina, making it easier to engage in daily activities and hobbies.

Improved mood: Addressing emotional challenges related to weight made my mood and social interactions better and helped manage depression and anxiety while hustling it out.

Better quality of life: By managing weight and maintaining physical and emotional health, I could improve my overall quality of life, making it possible to pursue personal and professional goals.

As someone who has experienced the negative effects of weight changes on physical health, I can confirm the effectiveness of these measures to enhance your overall well-being. By prioritizing self-care, adopting healthy eating habits, and making physical activity a regular part of my routine, I was able to shed extra kilos and become medication-free, something I never thought was possible.

It's important to remember that small changes lead to big results, and that taking care of yourself is not a selfish act, but a necessary one. By investing in your own health and well-being, you are not only benefiting yourself, but also those around you, as a healthier and happier you can positively impact the lives of others.

#2
Living with Chronic Illness: Coping & Conquering

On the Outside

Chronic illnesses are those that typically persist for a duration of a few months or years together. I have personally experienced the effects of a metabolic disorder that causes acute joint pain and hinders mobility. Through my friend Gout's help, I gained a better understanding of my body and how it functions. I discovered that chronic illnesses manifest as persistent symptoms that impacts our daily lives, including fatigue, inflammation, pain, and difficulty with daily activities. It's worth noting down that Heart disease, diabetes, and autoimmune disorders are among the leading causes of death worldwide.

Having a chronic illness leads to multiple challenges that affect how others perceive and engage with us. As someone who has personally experienced the impact of chronic illness and has witnessed it in my family and friends.

I have observed the following external challenges:

Physical Pain and Emotional Fear: Chronic illness brings physical pain and discomfort, hindering daily activities. It also leads to fear and uncertainty about the future, including concerns about disease progression and treatment.

Dependence on others: Chronic illness often results in physical limitations and the need for assistance with daily activities, which lead to dependence on others for support and care. When I experienced Gout flares, I was bedridden and relied on my wife for support and care, which affected her work life and increased her stress levels.

Social isolation: Chronic illness results in the need for frequent medical treatments, which can make it difficult to participate in social activities or maintain social connections. This can lead to feelings of loneliness and social isolation.

Workplace challenges: Chronic illness impacts workplace interactions, including how coworkers and supervisors perceive and interact with the individual. This can lead to challenges with job performance, promotions, and overall job satisfaction.

Financial strain: Chronic illness leads to significant financial strain due to increased medical expenses and missed work days.

Stigma and discrimination: Chronic illness can be stigmatized or misunderstood, leading to discrimination and negative stereotypes. This can impact how others view and interact with us, potentially leading to further isolation and marginalization.

Our body's signaling systems, such as pain, irritation, or swelling, let us know when there is harm caused to our external body or internal organs. Despite this, I have been guilty of taking shortcuts to numb those feelings and continue with the hustle of building my startup. Meanwhile, my wife developed Thyroid disorder after childbirth. Chronic health problems pose a big challenge in making it difficult to navigate daily life and maintain a positive sense of self.

On the Inside

Living with chronic health problems creates a sense of fear and uncertainty in our lives, regardless of age group. It not only affects us physically but also mentally and changes how we are perceived by friends and family. For students, it may affect their entrance exams, for professionals, it can impact their annual appraisal, promotions, and raises, and for those saving for a world tour, it can leave them grounded, the list doesn't end here. Overall it makes you feel small, weak, and can hit you hard.

As someone who have lived with chronic illness for over a decade, here are some of the underlying factors that have impacted my physical and emotional well-being and some others which i have not personally experienced but observed in my close circle:

Poor diet: Consuming a diet high in processed foods, sugar, and unhealthy fats leads to obesity, type 2 diabetes, heart disease, and other chronic illnesses.

Sedentary lifestyle: Lack of physical activity and prolonged sitting increase the risk of chronic illnesses such as heart disease, type 2 diabetes, and certain cancers.

Smoking and alcohol consumption: Smoking and excessive alcohol consumption increase the risk of developing several chronic illnesses, including cancer, heart disease, and liver disease.

Other Environmental factors: Exposure to toxins and pollutants in the air, water, and food leads to chronic illnesses such as cancer and respiratory diseases.

Genetics: Some chronic illnesses, such as certain types of cancer, have a genetic component that increases the risk of developing the disease.

Stress: Chronic stress has negative effects on the immune system, cardiovascular system, and other bodily systems, increasing the risk of chronic illnesses such as heart disease and depression.

Sleep deprivation: Chronic sleep deprivation weakens the immune system and increases the risk of developing chronic illnesses such as obesity, type 2 diabetes, and heart disease.

Living with chronic illness feels overwhelming and even hopeless at times. It can be easy to feel like there's no way to improve your situation. However, it's important to recognize that many of the underlying causes of chronic illness can be managed through lifestyle changes and mindful practices.

What Decisions do you need to consider?

After dealing with chronic illnesses in my family for over ten years, I have realized that a lot of them are caused by the choices we make in our daily lives. These choices include what we eat, how we exercise, how we sleep, our social activities, and hobbies. Our relationship with food has changed over time. Food, which was originally intended for nourishment and survival, has now become a source of comfort, entertainment, and even addiction due to the abundance and easy availability of food in our modern world.

Our brain's reward system is activated by both food and substances, which leads to cravings and the inability to control consumption. Overeating gives us temporary relief or distraction from uncomfortable feelings such as stress, anxiety, or depression.

Here are some decisions that worked well for me and can work for you too to cope and ultimately conquer chronic illness:

Create your new identity: To conquer chronic illness, it is important to create a new identity aligned with healthy habits. I am a follower of James Clear's "Atomic Habits". By focusing on our identity and who we want to become, we can build lasting habits that become a part of our daily lives.

Develop a support system: Living with chronic illness can be challenging, so it's important to develop a support system of friends, family members, or healthcare professionals who can provide emotional and physical support when needed.

Prioritize self-care: It's important to prioritize self-care and engage in activities that promote physical and emotional health, such as getting enough sleep, eating a healthy diet, and engaging in physical activity that is appropriate for the individual's limitations.

Communicate with healthcare professionals: Communication with healthcare professionals is key to managing chronic illness and coping with physical pain and emotional breakdown. It's important to discuss treatment options, potential side effects, and any concerns or questions with healthcare providers.

Find ways to cope with stress: Chronic illness causes emotional stress, so finding ways to cope with stress is important. Strategies such as mindfulness, meditation, or therapy helps you manage stress and maintain emotional well-being.

Explore adaptive technology and equipment: Adaptive technology and equipment help us with chronic illness manage physical limitations and engage in daily activities. It's important to explore options that can improve independence and quality of life such as wheelchairs, scooters, walkers, canes, crutches, prosthetic devices and so on.

Develop a plan for managing symptoms: Chronic illness causes physical symptoms that impact quality of life. Developing a plan for managing symptoms, such as pain, fatigue, or nausea, helps us better manage the condition and maintain physical and emotional health.

Suffering and enduring pain is something nobody enjoys, and when faced with a chronic illness, it's easy to overlook its long-term effects. Neglecting to address the root cause of the problem can worsen the underlying condition. That's why it's crucial to be attentive and mindful of our body's signals. This enables us to seek professional help or self-help to identify the problem early on. In my case, I was informed that I had to take gout medication for life. However, by making changes to my lifestyle, I was able to manage my levels and pass my blood tests with flying colors.

Therefore, it's essential to prioritize self-care by engaging in regular physical activity, adopting a healthy diet, and managing stress while getting adequate sleep to promote overall health and well-being. By making these decisions and taking proactive steps towards managing chronic illness, adapting to physical changes and limitations, individuals can improve their overall well-being and quality of life.

What Results you can hope to see:

I found our healthcare system is focused on treating symptoms, rather than addressing the root cause of the problem. This results in a lack of emphasis on the importance of self-care and the impact of our lifestyle choices on our overall health. We're expected to pay three times: for the doctor's visit, for lab tests, and for prescription medication. We often forget that our body is an accumulation of what we have acquired, such as the food we eat, the air we breathe, and the water we drink. It's essential to understand that we become what we consume.

Our body is nothing less than a high-end Ferrari, and it's sophisticated. Just as we wouldn't put anything into our Ferrari, we should be mindful of what we put into our bodies. Unfortunately, many of us neglect our bodies and then complain about the pain, gas, bloating, and other signals that our body sends us. It's important to realize that what we consume has a direct impact on our health.

After discovering how to cope and conquer my chronic illness, I could experience the following:

Improved physical health: As a result of managing my chronic illness and improving my physical health, I felt a sense of lightness, fluidity, and flow. My symptoms had a reduced impact on my daily life, and I could experience improved physical health.

Increased self-esteem and body image: Addressing emotional challenges related to chronic illness improved my self-esteem and body image, leading to greater confidence and overall mental health.

Better relationships: By addressing emotional challenges related to chronic illness, I could improve the ability to connect with others and build healthy relationships.

Increased energy and stamina: By engaging in activities that promote physical health, such as exercise and good sleep habits, I could increase my energy and stamina, making it easier to engage in daily activities, playing with kids and pursuing hobbies.

Improved mood: By being more mindful of what I eat and staying present in the moment, I was able to manage stress and improve my mood. I no longer experienced extreme highs and lows throughout the day.

Better quality of life: By managing chronic illness and adapting to physical changes and limitations, individuals can improve their overall quality of life, making it easier to pursue personal and professional goals.

While not all chronic illnesses can be managed through lifestyle changes, I believe that the majority can be. By making conscious decisions about what we eat, engaging in regular exercise, and managing stress, we can improve our overall health and well-being. Of course, it's always essential to seek advice from healthcare professionals for those chronic illnesses that require medical intervention.

Overall, by taking proactive steps towards managing chronic illness and adapting to physical changes and limitations, we can experience a range of positive results that will improve our overall well-being and quality of life.

#3

Technology and Your Physical Health: How Screen Time Affects Your Body

On the Outside

My work and hobbies both revolve around screens. During my college days, I spent non-stop 8-12 hours playing video games in pro leagues on a CRT flat monitor. Even after my gaming sessions, I would spend another 2-3 hours on my favorite Nokia Symbian devices. After I began working in the IT industry, my screen time only increased, although I could no longer play games for as long. Instead, the office monitor replaced my gaming time. With time, I began experiencing watery eyes and when I went to see a doctor, I was diagnosed with dry eye syndrome.

These are the some of the common physical symptoms that can result from excessive screen time:

Eye strain and dry eyes: Prolonged screen time makes our eyes feel tired, dry, and irritated. It can also cause headaches.

Poor posture: Spending too much time hunched over a screen leads to neck and back pain, which can make you feel uncomfortable and affect your posture.

Sleep disturbances: Using screens late at night makes it harder for us to fall asleep, leading to fatigue and difficulty concentrating during the day.

Weight gain: Being glued to our screen for long periods can make us more sedentary and less likely to engage in physical activity, which leads to weight gain.

Reduced physical activity: Spending too much time on screens displaces physical activity and leads to a reduction in overall physical activity levels.

Increased risk of repetitive strain injuries: Using electronic devices for prolonged periods leads to pain and discomfort in our hands, wrists, and arms. Some common injuries include carpal tunnel syndrome, tendinitis, tennis elbow, and trigger finger.

On the Inside:

A significant part of human evolution has revolved around finding food and protecting ourselves from becoming prey. As social beings, we have a natural longing for togetherness, which has manifested itself in various ways throughout history. In modern times, especially in cities, there's a rat race to make more money in order to live a high-quality life. Unfortunately, in pursuit of our future goals, we often ignore the present.

If your profession demands screen-time, finding an alternate profession may not be a practical solution. With digitization, every industry and interface are rapidly becoming digital, and screens are almost unavoidable. We need to learn how to use screens to our advantage while also prioritizing our health.

Millennials who were born in the 1980s have been using digital technology for the longest duration compared to other generations. As we continue to evolve as a species, it will be fascinating to witness the challenge of integrating screens into our lives while still prioritizing our physical and mental well-being.

Excessive screen time have various underlying root causes that impact physical health, including:

> **Sedentary lifestyle**: Prolonged screen time leads to a sedentary lifestyle, where individuals may be sitting for extended periods and not engaging in physical activity.
>
> **Blue light exposure**: The blue light emitted by screens affects the natural sleep cycle by suppressing the production of the hormone melatonin, leading to sleep disturbances and disruptions to circadian rhythms.
>
> **Poor posture**: Poor posture while using electronic devices leads to neck and back pain, which can be chronic and affect overall physical health.
>
> **Reduced physical activity**: Time spent on screens displaces physical activity, leading to a reduction in overall physical activity levels.
>
> **Addiction**: Screen time addiction leads to a lack of self-control and excessive use, which negatively impacts physical health and overall well-being.
>
> **Stress and anxiety**: Constant notifications, emails, and messages leads to increased stress and anxiety, which have a negative impact on physical health over time.

It is important to recognize these underlying root causes and take steps to mitigate their negative impact on physical health by engaging in physical activity, maintaining good posture, reducing screen time, and practicing stress management techniques.

What Decisions do you need to consider?

The first decision I considered for myself was accepting the fact that my professional and personal development can't happen without screen-time and long exposure to screen light. It also means that to get any productive work done, I need to focus and concentrate and that means I need to sit in one place for long hours. You see the first step to change starts when you accept what cannot be changed. I started to read, listen and experiment with myself and my team on better posture, screen filters and natural light. If you are working in a big corporation, or studying in a fancy college there are high chances this is already well thought and executed. For my startup I had to figure it out myself and learn by experimenting.

Consider the following solutions when addressing issues concerning technology and your physical health, particularly with regards to screen time and its impact on your body.

Sure, here are some decisions to consider when mitigating the negative impact of excessive screen time on physical health:

Time management - Social media apps and games are designed to keep you engaged, so it's important to prioritize important activities. You can use screen monitoring tools to track where your time is going and the 80/20 rule to cut back on mindless activities.

Screen adjustments - In the past, we used to protect eyes from the harmful effects of CRT monitors by installing blue protective glass on all office screens. Nowadays, we can adjust our screen settings to "Night mode" to reduce blue light exposure, much like wearing blue light blocking glasses.

Posture - One way to maintain good posture is to imagine a vertical line running through your body, ensuring proper alignment - a technique known as the "plumb line". Sit with your back straight, feet flat on the ground, and shoulders relaxed. Monitor should be at or slightly below your eye level.

Regular breaks - Use the Pomodoro technique to take regular breaks from screen time, I find working for 50 mins at a stretch with 10 mins break most productive for me.

Screen-free zones - Establishing screen-free zones or times during the day, such as during meals or in certain rooms of the house, helped reduce screen time and promote more meaningful activities and interactions.

Stress management - To manage stress, incorporate mindfulness meditation into your routine and set aside sacred hours for self-care and family without being interrupted by notifications and alerts, while also learning to compartmentalize different aspects of your life.

Professional help - Seeking professional help or counseling can be helpful in managing the negative impacts of screen time on your physical and mental health. It's better to take proactive medical intervention rather than waiting for the problem to become too severe to handle.

What Results you can hope to see:

Effective management of screen time doesn't guarantee success, but it prepares us to adapt to the changes required in this fast-changing technological era. Nowadays, kids use screen devices effortlessly without any training, as it has become a natural part of their environment. However, self-awareness and self-control are crucial in using screens as a tool instead of becoming addicted to them. The future's successful leaders will be those who not only consume screen devices and apps but also create them.

Here are some potential results that one can hope to see after implementing decisions to mitigate the negative impact of excessive screen time on physical health:

Reduced eye strain and improved vision: By adjusting screen settings, practicing good posture, and taking regular breaks from screen time, we can reduce eye strain and improve their overall vision.

Reduced neck and back pain: By practicing good posture and taking regular breaks from screen time, one can reduce chronic neck and back pain associated with excessive screen time.

Improved sleep quality: By reducing blue light exposure before bedtime and taking regular breaks from screen time, one can improve their sleep quality and quantity.

Reduced stress and anxiety: By practicing stress management techniques and taking regular breaks from screen time, one can reduce stress and anxiety associated with excessive screen time.

Improved overall physical health: By prioritizing other activities over screen time, engaging in regular physical exercise, and adopting a healthy lifestyle, one can improve their overall physical health and well-being.

Technology has brought numerous benefits to our lives, but it is important to recognize the negative impact it can have on our physical and mental health. From screen time to posture, stress management to time management, there are various ways to mitigate the effects of technology on our bodies. By being mindful of our habits and taking proactive steps to address any issues that arise, we can live healthier and happier lives in our increasingly digital world. Remember, it's all about finding a balance that works for you and your unique needs.

#4

Changing Sleep Patterns: How it Impacts Your Physical Health

On the Outside

In my quest to achieve peak performance I have come to learn that rest and recovery is crucial, with sleep being one of the most important factors. Interestingly sleep contributes to our physical growth during childhood and adolescence by releasing growth hormone, it no longer affects our height after physical development is complete. Nevertheless, our body still requires sleep for maintenance work, and as we age and go through different life stages, our sleep patterns vary. I have come to understand that the number of hours we sleep isn't the only important factor, but the quality of our sleep plays a crucial role in our overall physical health.

As we go through different life stages, our sleep patterns can vary greatly. During infancy and childhood, we tend to sleep for longer periods and have more REM sleep, which is crucial for brain development. As we enter adolescence, our sleep patterns may shift due to changes in our circadian rhythm, leading to later bedtimes and difficulty waking up early for school. As adults, work and family responsibilities may disrupt our sleep patterns, leading to insomnia or sleep deprivation. And as we age, our sleep may become lighter and more fragmented, leading to more frequent awakenings during the night.

Due to the changing sleep patterns and poor sleep quality I could experience a range of physical health problems such as:

Dark circles and puffiness around the eyes

Skin problems like acne, eczema, and premature aging

Hair loss or thinning

Difficulty in concentration and memory problems

Reduced productivity and increased irritability

Increased risk of accidents due to drowsiness and fatigue

Weight gain or difficulty in losing weight

Weakened immune system leading to frequent illnesses

Hormonal imbalances, including irregular periods and decreased libido

Increased risk of chronic health conditions, including cardiovascular disease, diabetes, and depression.

On the Inside:

During my childhood, I used to live with my grandparents and sleep early as per their routine. However, when I moved to Chennai for studies and started living alone, I began staying up late at night to watch movies, play video games, and socialize with my room-mates. This habit continued throughout my college days and later, during my startup days with my team, as we worked tirelessly to bring our vision to life. Now, with a young 1 year old second child, we struggle to maintain a consistent sleep pattern due to his erratic sleep cycle.

Due to changing sleep patterns over the years, both as an individual and as a family, I have experienced several problems that have affected my physical and emotional well-being.

Stress and anxiety: These led to difficulty in falling asleep, staying asleep, or achieving restful sleep altogether.

Medical conditions: Chronic pain, sleep apnea, and restless leg syndrome are examples of medical conditions that can cause sleep disturbances.

Lifestyle factors: Alcohol and caffeine consumption, irregular sleep schedules, and lack of physical activity can all affect sleep quality.

Environmental factors: Noise, light, and temperature can all affect sleep quality.

Aging: As we age, our sleep patterns tend to change, and we may experience more frequent awakenings during the night.

Genetics: Certain genetic factors may influence sleep patterns and quality.

Medications: Some medications can interfere with sleep, including those for high blood pressure, depression, and asthma.

All of these factors contribute to changing sleep patterns and poor sleep quality, which can then lead to a range of physical and mental health problems. Therefore, it is crucial to identify and address the underlying causes of sleep disturbances to improve overall health and well-being.

What Decisions do you need to consider?

As someone who used to have arguments with my wife without any explanation, I later realized it was due to high stress levels from overworking and lack of sleep. I learned that sleep is essential for both physical and emotional well-being, and we should prioritize it as much as eating healthy and exercising. Developing a consistent sleep routine that aligns with our natural sleep rhythms is crucial to improving overall health.

Based on my experience, here are some important decisions to consider when addressing the impact of changing sleep patterns on physical health.

Establish a regular sleep schedule: Establishing a regular sleep schedule to help regulate the body's circadian rhythm, leading to better sleep quality and improved physical and emotional health.

Prioritize sleep hygiene: Prioritizing sleep hygiene, such as avoiding screens before bedtime, avoiding caffeine and alcohol before bedtime, and creating a comfortable sleep environment, can help improve sleep quality and promote overall health.

Seek treatment for sleep disorders: If experiencing sleep disorders, it's important to seek treatment from a healthcare professional to identify and manage the underlying causes of sleep disturbance.

Engage in physical activity: Engaging in regular physical activity to improve sleep quality and promote overall physical and emotional health.

Manage stress: Managing stress through strategies such as mindfulness, meditation, or therapy improves our sleep quality and promotes overall well-being.

Consult with a healthcare professional: Consulting with a healthcare professional can help identify any underlying health conditions that may be contributing to sleep disturbances and develop a personalized plan for managing them.

As I have learned from my own experience, considering the decisions mentioned above and taking proactive steps towards managing changing sleep patterns and promoting physical and emotional health significantly improves our overall well-being and quality of life. It's important to prioritize sleep and address any underlying causes of sleep disturbances to ensure that we are functioning at our best. By doing so, we live a more fulfilling and enjoyable life.

What Results you can hope to see:

I've had some of my best breakthroughs when stuck with problems of building scalable products and going to the market after getting a good night's sleep. Just like we defragment computer hard disks for better performance and speed, sleep does the same to our brains. By being mindful of my own sleep, I realized I am not a night person and found my rhythm by taking up the hardest problem to solve first thing in the morning. It's important to find your own sleep rhythm and deep work time when you are least distracted and highly productive, whether you are a student, professional, or med-senior executive, as this can be a productivity powerhouse for you.

Addressing the problems related to changing sleep patterns and their impact on our physical health lead to several positive outcomes, including:

Improved physical health: By managing changing sleep patterns and improving sleep quality, we can improve our physical health, reduce the risk of health complications, and increase energy levels.

Better mood: Improved sleep quality can positively impact our mood, reducing the risk of depression and anxiety. This in turn can create a more positive atmosphere at home and work, improving overall well-being and productivity.

Increased cognitive function: By improving sleep quality, we can improve our cognitive functions, including concentration, memory, and problem-solving skills.

Better productivity: Improved sleep quality can lead to better productivity at work and in daily life.

Improved relationships: Improved sleep quality leads to better relationships by reducing irritability, improving mood, and increasing energy levels.

Better quality of life: By managing changing sleep patterns and improving sleep quality, we can improve our overall quality of life, making it easier to pursue personal and professional goals.

There are many factors that can impact our sleep patterns and quality of sleep, but by being mindful of our habits and making intentional decisions to prioritize sleep, we can experience a range of benefits. From improved mood and reduced risk of depression and anxiety, to better physical health and more productive days, sleep plays a crucial role in our overall well-being. By taking proactive steps towards managing sleep, we can create a more fulfilling and satisfying life.

#5

Aging Gracefully: Navigating Physical Change as You Grow Older

On the Outside:

Watching my parents age and my children grow up, I am reminded of how our bodies change over time. When my second child was born, I witnessed firsthand how a rapidly growing body and mind can lead to disrupted sleep patterns. More recently, I saw how my 70-year-old father's mind was ready to climb the 740 steps to Vaishno Devi, but his body was not able to keep up with his mind.

As we age, our bodies undergo changes both internally and externally, and it's not always reflected in our chronological age. Biological age is a measure of how well our body functions as compared to our chronological age, and can be influenced by factors such as genetics, lifestyle, and environmental factors. Even if we are young chronologically, if our body is biologically aged, it can have a significant impact on our physical health and well-being. This can manifest in several ways, such as decreased mobility, disrupted sleep patterns, and increased risk of chronic diseases.

I've realized the importance of aging gracefully and navigating physical changes that come with age.

However, it can lead to various external issues that affect how people perceive and interact with us, including:

> **Ageism**: Aging leads to negative stereotypes and discrimination based on age, which can impact how others view and interact with the individual. This leads to challenges with job opportunities, access to healthcare, and social connections.
>
> **Financial strain:** Aging leads to increased medical expenses and decreased ability to work, leading to financial strain and potential challenges with access to healthcare and other resources.

Changes in social roles: Aging results in changes in social roles, such as retirement, which impacts how others view and interact with the individual. This can lead to challenges with maintaining social connections and finding a sense of purpose.

Dependence on others: Aging leads to physical limitations or the need for assistance with daily activities, which can lead to dependence on others for support and care.

Safety concerns: Falls are the second leading cause of unintentional injury deaths worldwide as per WHO. Aging leads to safety concerns, such as increased risk of falls and life-threatening injury.

Seeking support and resources to manage aging gracefully is crucial for us to navigate daily life and maintain a positive sense of self. By prioritizing physical and emotional health, we can improve our overall well-being and enjoy a better quality of life as we age.

On the Inside:

Did you know that on average, the cells in your body are replaced every 7 to 10 years? That means every decade, you are physically a new person. But what about our minds? As we age, our brains accumulate both good and bad memories. While these memories can give us the experience and wisdom to handle life's challenges, they can also weigh us down with painful memories of past traumas or regrets.

The aging process leads to various underlying causes that affect our physical and emotional health.

Some underlying causes related to aging include:

Physical discomfort and pain: Aging causes physical discomfort, pain, and other symptoms that impacts our ability to function and engage in daily activities.

Emotional stress: It also causes emotional stress, including anxiety, depression, or stress related to managing the impact on daily life and overall health.

Loss of identity: Our sense of identity, leading to feelings of loss and difficulty adapting to changes in physical ability and limitations.

Fatigue and lack of energy: As we age, fatigue and lack of energy become more common, which can negatively affect our ability to carry out daily activities and maintain relationships.

Uncertainty and fear: Aging causes uncertainty and fear about the future, including concerns about health complications, financial stability, and overall well-being.

Self-esteem and body image: Aging impacts our self-esteem and body image, leading to negative emotions and feelings of inadequacy.

As we age, our bodies undergo several changes, the primary being fatigue and lack of energy. These impact our ability to engage in daily activities and maintain relationships, highlighting the importance of prioritizing self-care and seeking support when needed. Seeking support from friends, family members, or a professional counselor helps us address emotional challenges related to aging gracefully.

What Decisions do you need to consider?

As we age, our bodies undergo various physical changes that can impact our overall well-being. It's natural to feel apprehensive about these changes and wonder how we can navigate them gracefully. One approach to addressing physical changes is through the Japanese concept of ikigai, or "the reason for being". Ken Mogi, a neuroscientist and happiness expert, suggests considering if an activity aligns with the five pillars that allow your ikigai to thrive: feeling fulfilled, doing the work, growth and improvement, avoiding affirmation delusion, and taking positive action. By making decisions that align with our ikigai, we can continue to live a fulfilling life as we age.

"When I was 20, I wanted to be a millionaire ... Now that I'm a millionaire, I want to be 20."

~ Alex Hormozi.

Here are some decisions to consider when attempting to solve problems related to aging gracefully and navigating physical change as you grow older:

Prioritize self-care: Prioritizing self-care, including engaging in physical activity, eating a healthy diet, and practicing stress-reducing techniques such as mindfulness or meditation, helps maintain physical and emotional health.

Maintain social connections: Maintaining social connections and finding ways to engage in meaningful activities helps combat feelings of isolation and maintain a sense of purpose. Try to spend time with people half your age, it helps you learn new things, gain new perspectives and stay mentally agile.

Consult with a healthcare professional: Consulting with a healthcare professional helps identify any underlying health conditions and develop a personalized plan for managing physical changes and maintaining overall health.

Explore options for independence: One way to maintain independence as we age is to explore different options, such as modifying our homes or using mobility aids. By doing so, we can continue to have a sense of control over our lives and maintain our overall quality of life.

Seek support and resources: Seeking support from friends, family members, or a professional counselor to address emotional challenges related to aging gracefully and maintain overall well-being.

As we journey through life, our body is the vehicle that carries us through all our activities and experiences. Neglecting our physical health as we age can make life challenging. By making conscious decisions and taking proactive steps to manage physical changes and prioritize both physical and emotional health, we can improve our overall well-being and quality of life. As we age, it's crucial to seek support and resources to manage physical changes, maintain a positive sense of self, and remain engaged in meaningful activities.

What Results you can hope to see:

Coming from humble beginnings myself, I've realized that in our youth, we often have the abundance of time and health but lack financial stability. As we start our careers, we may have more financial security but little time and our health may begin to suffer. However, as we age, our health becomes a top priority as we strive to preserve and reverse the aging process through proper care and common sense. This is a unique time in our lives to experience and give back to society, which can provide immense fulfillment and happiness. Ultimately, it's not about the length of our lives, but the impact we have on others.

There are several positive results that you can hope to see once you have navigated physical changes as you grow older:

Improved physical health: By managing physical changes and prioritizing physical health, we can improve our overall physical health, maintain independence, and reduce the risk of health complications.

Better mental health: By addressing emotional challenges related to aging gracefully, we can improve our mental health, reduce the risk of depression and anxiety, and maintain a positive outlook on life.

Increased social connections: By maintaining social connections and engaging in meaningful activities, we can reduce feelings of isolation and maintain a sense of purpose.

Better quality of life: By prioritizing self-care and adapting to physical changes, we can maintain a good quality of life, find joy and meaning in the aging process, and maintain our independence.

Financial stability: By taking proactive steps towards financial stability, we can help ensure that we are able to enjoy our later years with confidence and peace of mind.

Taking proactive steps towards managing physical and emotional health is a priority we can't ignore. By doing so, we experience a range of positive outcomes, including improved energy levels, better mood, and greater financial stability. Ultimately, aging gracefully is about maintaining our sense of purpose, staying connected to others, and taking care of our bodies and minds as we navigate the challenges and opportunities that come with growing older. We are the actors and directors of our own "It's a Wonderful Life" movie.

Ready starters for this Chapter to start implementing:

(Scan this QR for Mental Models, Links to Proven Frameworks and Excel templates to get started)

5

MENTAL AND CHANGE

The human mind is a double-edged sword. On one hand, it has the power to create beautiful dreams, and on the other, it could drown in the darkness of past mistakes. For years, my mind was like a rudderless ship. It was constantly haunted by the ghosts of my past. I couldn't escape the memories, the regrets, and the never-ending cycle of "what ifs". Later I realized I had to learn to let go and forgive, not just others, but also myself. This was perhaps the first step towards my personal transformation.

When I began to release myself from the grip of my past, I discovered that my mind was still uncertain, influenced more by memories than by actual experiences. Factors such as my background, upbringing, small-town mindset, and not being friends with high achievers in school shaped my belief system. I was living a life based on what I thought I knew, instead of trying to better understand my own mental state. It was time for me to leave my comfort zone and welcome new learnings and experiences.

Through practicing meditation and manifestation, my imagination often carried me away to an idealized future. I started creating my manifestation scrapbook with a lot of love. But I was never able to find the courage to act upon those dreams. It took me time to realize that the only way to come out of my situation is by acting in the present, for it was the only way to turn those dreams into reality.

The words of Dr. Leland Kaiser resonated with me: "You can change your future as quickly as you can change your mind." I discovered that the key to unlocking my true potential lay in the power of my thoughts. By cultivating a growth mindset, I could transform my life, overcome my limitations, and achieve the goals I once thought were unattainable.

Reflecting on my journey, I am filled with gratitude and face the future with determination. I am no longer held back by my past or passively daydreaming. Instead, I actively engage in my own life, embracing mental growth and change as I shape my destiny with each thought and action.

Some key topics on how changes impact our mental being

#1. Change and Trauma: How to Manage the Psychological Aftermath

#2. Navigating Change as a Family: Supporting Each Other's Mental Health

#3. Loneliness in the Digital Age: How Technology Is Changing Our Sense of Connection and Isolation.

#4. Moving On: The Psychological Impacts of Relocation and How to Cope

#5. Relationship Changes and Mental Health: Navigating Breakups and Divorces

#1
Change and Trauma: How to Manage the Psychological Aftermath

On the Outside

We often joked during college that Chennai had three seasons: hot, hotter, and hottest. It was on a sweltering, sunny morning, I took my girlfriend for a ride on an old scooter to a nearby ATM. Unfortunately, the scooter tipped over on the freshly laid, sharp-edged tarmac. In my attempt to protect her and safely land the scooter, I suffered a severe injury to my left foot. A 5-inch by 3-inch patch of flesh was torn away, loosely hanging from my leg. I was bleeding profusely. My final year Polytechnic exams were just a week away.

Trauma, like the accident I experienced, can significantly affect our lives and lead to changes in the way we perceive and interact with the world. The psychological aftermath of such events manifests in various forms, such as anxiety, fear, or even post-traumatic stress disorder (PTSD). These mental and emotional reactions influence our daily activities, relationships, and decision-making processes, sometimes making it difficult to move forward and adapt to new circumstances.

When traumatic events happen, we see and experience things differently that influence how we cope with the situation.

Here are some of them:

Triggers: Certain places, sounds, or smells can remind us of the trauma we may have faced, making us feel anxious or upset. I did not touch a scooty for a long time after my accident.

Behavior changes: People who have faced trauma might act differently, like becoming quieter, more irritable, or taking part in risky activities.

Support from others: Having a support system of friends, family, or support groups can greatly impact how we cope with trauma. In my case, thanks to my girlfriend's love and care, I was able to gather myself and even make it to final year exams in an ambulance.

Media coverage: The media coverage of large-scale traumatic events, such as natural disasters or acts of violence, can intensify the emotional impact experienced by us. I have observed my father-in-law getting deeply affected by news flashbacks related to the India partition in 1947.

Social stigma: Sometimes, we might feel judged or looked down upon for experiencing trauma or struggling with mental health, which make it harder to talk about or seek help. Some may adapt their behavior or hide their struggles to fit societal expectations.

Cultural influences: I have come to understand how cultural beliefs and attitudes towards trauma, mental health, and healing can greatly influence one's personal experiences and their approach to seeking help. For example, I chose not to reveal the details of my traumatic accident to my parents until after my exams because I feared they might take me back home, hindering my ability to take the exams.

On the Inside

There are various types of traumas that can affect our psychological well-being. Interpersonal trauma, contrary to what the media often depicts, does not discriminate based on gender. Instead, it revolves around an imbalance of power, trust, or influence.

In my own experience, I was physically abused by my neighbor aunt & her friends where my grandmother sent me to spend time with after school. The distressing events continued for years until I recognized the situation and stopped visiting their place, feeling both ashamed and upset.

It is essential to consider the underlying root causes that contribute to the development of traumatic responses.

Some common root causes include:

Loss of safety: Traumatic events often involve a sense of losing safety or security, which can lead to a heightened state of fear or anxiety.

Powerlessness: Experiencing a traumatic event causes feelings of helplessness or powerlessness, in my case I was unable to control or prevent the situation.

Betrayal: In cases where trauma involves interpersonal relationships, such as abuse or neglect, feelings of betrayal can be profound, especially when the perpetrator is someone trusted or relied upon as my neighbor aunt.

Shame and guilt: Survivors of traumatic events feel shame or guilt, either as a result of being unable to prevent the event or due to a misguided belief that they are somehow responsible for what happened. I lived with this shame and guilt for half of my life.

Disrupted attachment: Early childhood trauma, such as abuse or neglect, disrupts the formation of secure attachments, leading to difficulties with trust and emotional regulation later in life. I still somehow feel people will take advantage of me and move on.

Identity challenges: Traumatic events cause us to question our sense of self, leading to identity challenges and difficulties in establishing a stable sense of self-worth. I chose to leave for Chennai for higher studies after my 10th to find my own identity where none knew me.

Biological factors: The more I studied, I found the body's stress response system, including the release of stress hormones like cortisol and adrenaline, can be significantly impacted by trauma. This leads to changes in brain chemistry and function, which in turn affects emotional regulation, memory, and other cognitive processes.

It's important to acknowledge the complexity of trauma and work towards understanding its root causes, as this is an essential step towards the healing and recovery process.

What Decisions do you need to consider?

As I reflect on my journey, I realize that being an introverted person has taught me valuable lessons. Embracing my vulnerability and accepting myself wholeheartedly has allowed me to move past my traumatic experiences. I feel grateful for the non-judgmental friends who have listened and supported me.

I've learned that seeking help from mental health professionals is an important step towards healing, and it's not something to be ashamed of. Ultimately, my goal was to be happy, and this couldn't be achieved without addressing and overcoming my past traumas. Overcoming the psychological aftermath of trauma is a difficult and complex process.

There are several important decisions that I needed to consider in this journey:

Practicing self-care: Trauma takes a toll on our mental and physical health, and prioritizing self-care activities such as exercise, meditation, and healthy eating greatly helps reduce stress and promote well-being.

Seeking professional help: Trauma affects various aspects of our lives, and seeking the help of a mental health professional can be instrumental in addressing the issues and finding effective coping mechanisms. I tried to do it myself, and wasted valuable years.

Creating a support system: It's essential to have a support system of people who are non-judgmental, empathetic, and understanding. Whether it's friends, family, or a support group, having a network of people to rely on makes a significant difference.

Processing and expressing emotions: It's essential to process and express emotions safely and constructively. This can involve journaling, art therapy, or talking with a trusted friend or professional.

Adopting a growth mindset: Instead of viewing trauma as a permanent state, it can be helpful to adopt a growth mindset that focuses on learning and development. This involves recognizing that recovery is a process, and it takes time to achieve lasting healing and growth.

The process of healing is unique to each individual, and it requires time, effort, and patience. Ultimately, the goal is to move towards healing, growth, and well-being for happiness.

What Results you can hope to see:

Once I had overcome my past traumas, I found myself feeling lost and directionless for a period of time. It was as though I had to take a few steps back before making a big leap forward. However, the process of self-transformation that followed was truly life-changing. By changing my belief system, I found that it changed the way I looked at things and approached life.

Some of the positive changes that we can hope to see as a result of the healing process include:

Improved mental and physical health: Overcoming trauma led to improvements in overall mental and physical health, including reduced anxiety, depression, and stress. More importantly, I learnt how to cope and deal with it later in my life. More recently the process helped me cope with my mother's demise.

Greater self-awareness: By processing and expressing emotions, we can gain a greater understanding of ourselves, the triggers, and how to manage our emotions and increase awareness.

Stronger relationships: Building a support system of non-judgmental and empathetic individuals helps strengthen relationships and promote social connectedness.

Increased resilience: Adopting a growth mindset and learning effective coping mechanisms increases our resilience and improves the ability to navigate future challenges.

Greater sense of purpose and meaning: Overcoming trauma leads to a renewed sense of purpose and meaning in life, and a greater appreciation for the present moment.

Ultimately, it's important to accept what has happened in the past, act in the present, and determine the future we want for ourselves. Staying stuck and replaying the same thoughts and emotions over and over again only serves to hold us back. We need to find the strength to break free from the chains of our past and liberate ourselves to live a life that is free, open, and independent.

By overcoming the psychological aftermath of trauma, we can achieve improvements in overall well-being, greater self-awareness, stronger relationships, increased resilience, and a greater sense of purpose and meaning in life.

#2

Navigating Change as a Family: Supporting Each Other's Mental Health

On the Outside

Navigating change as a family and supporting each other's mental health has been challenging in our family. Personally, I have realized that external influences, such as societal pressures, the influence of colleagues, the communities we are a part of, and even the schools our children attend impact our overall well-being.

After getting married, the dynamics within our family, including power dynamics and communication styles with my parents, posed additional challenges in navigating change together. When my wife became pregnant, especially during the birth of our first child, she experienced heightened emotional vulnerability. As our children grew older, we discovered that providing the necessary mental support for their growth became increasingly demanding for us.

Several such factors can lead to challenges when navigating change as a family and supporting each other's mental health:

> **Societal expectations and norms**: Society has certain expectations for how families should function, and these expectations impact family dynamics and mental health. For example, gender roles, work-life balance expectations, and parenting norms created stress or conflict within our family.
>
> **Economic factors**: Financial stress and job instability strains the family relationships and affect mental health. Economic challenges lead to difficult decisions, such as relocating for work, which may disrupt family routines and create additional stress.
>
> **Education**: Our education system and schools also influence family dynamics and mental health. Issues like academic pressure, social

expectations, and extracurricular activities create stress for both children and parents.

Health-related issues: Chronic illnesses, disabilities, or mental health disorders within the family create additional stress and require families to adapt and navigate change.

Community and social support: The availability and quality of community resources and social support systems can influence how families manage change and support each other's mental health. Limited access to mental health services, child care, and community support can make it more challenging for families to cope with changes.

Cultural factors: Different cultural beliefs and practices influence family dynamics, expectations, and mental health. Navigating change may be more difficult if a family's cultural background conflicts with mainstream societal norms.

Major life events: Life events such as marriage, divorce, birth, death, or job loss can trigger significant changes within a family. These events impact family dynamics and require adaptation to new circumstances, which can be challenging for mental health.

In the intricate web of family dynamics and societal pressures, navigating change and providing mental health support for each other becomes a complex and delicate challenge. Recognizing these multifaceted external factors is crucial to fostering understanding, empathy, and resilience within families as they face life's inevitable transitions.

On the Inside

In the Dunbar circle, family forms the innermost circle, being the closest and dearest to us. We rely on them without hesitation or doubt. However, as we live our urban lives, we rarely gather to share our struggles and engage in deeper conversations. In modern Indian cities, nuclear families are becoming increasingly common. The younger generation is pressed for time, while the older generation yearns for conversation, finally free after years of work. To raise children, we rely on daycare providers and tutors, who often know more about our kids than we do ourselves. We must not ignore the deeper problems and underlying causes of psychological and mental health issues within families. Ultimately, we return to our family, and we are responsible for creating the home environment in which we live.

The root causes of struggles in mental health and family dynamics will vary from family to family.

Some common internal factors I have come across include:

Communication breakdown: Poor communication within the family leads to misunderstandings, misinterpretations, and a lack of emotional support. This causes frustration and increased stress, further straining relationships.

Unresolved conflicts: Longstanding unresolved conflicts or disputes within a family leads to tension, resentment, and emotional distance, impacting the overall well-being of family members.

Family role expectations: Preconceived notions about family roles and responsibilities can create pressure and stress, leading to conflict and a lack of emotional support within the family.

Parenting styles: Differing parenting styles or beliefs causes disagreement and strain relationships between partners or between parents and children.

Mental health issues: Undiagnosed or untreated mental health issues can affect a person's behavior, emotions, and relationships with family members. This creates an unstable environment and leads to further mental health challenges.

Substance abuse: Substance abuse by a family member can disrupt the family dynamic, create instability, and lead to emotional turmoil. I have seen this happen in close quarters and it can be tragic to the whole family.

Past trauma: Unresolved traumas from past experiences influence a person's emotions, behaviors, and reactions within the family dynamic, potentially leading to conflicts or mental health challenges.

Emotional neglect: A lack of emotional support or validation within the family leads to feelings of isolation, loneliness, and low self-esteem, all of which contributes to mental health struggles.

Peeling back the layers to uncover the root causes of family struggles is a complex yet crucial endeavor. In doing so, we pave the way for healing, growth, and stronger connections that foster a nurturing family environment.

What Decisions do you need to consider?

We moved from Chennai to Kolkata so our parents could help raise our kids in a familiar Bengali setting. We had to deal with the challenges of adjusting to both sets of in-laws. Like new workplace teams, our families went through the stages: forming, storming, norming, and finally performing. We had big fights, with clashing values, lifestyles, and mindsets between our parents. One important thing we learned was to accept what we couldn't change, especially with the older family members. So, my wife and I accepted our parents with their unique values, backgrounds, and personalities. This helped us move from the storming stage to the norming stage.

For supporting each other's mental health and navigating change as a family, think about the following decisions:

Open communication: This is the key. Prioritize honest, open, and non-judgmental communication to better understand each other's needs and feelings.

Family meetings: This is not your daily agile scrum call! Having casual and informal family meetings is important to discuss issues, changes, and ways to support one another. The role of a facilitator holds the key here.

Professional help: Decide whether to seek professional guidance from a therapist, counselor, or support group to help navigate changes and address mental health concerns in the family especially in the case of substance abuse or trauma related.

Educate and raise awareness: Commit to learning more about mental health and sharing this knowledge with family members to reduce stigma and improve understanding.

Establish boundaries: Determine and enforce healthy boundaries within the family to ensure mutual respect and maintain emotional well-being.

Adapt to cultural differences: Be open to understanding and accepting cultural differences within the family, finding ways to respect and incorporate these differences into family life.

Support networks: Decide to build and maintain social support networks outside the family, such as friends, neighbors, or community groups, to provide additional emotional support.

Time management: Prioritize family time. Find a balance between work, family life, and self-care, allowing space for supporting each other's mental health.

Addressing conflicts: Develop a plan for addressing and resolving conflicts within the family, promoting a healthy environment for change and mental health support.

As social beings, we need a place to vent out our frustrations, emotions, and stress. Work together as a family to create a supportive and open environment, and develop healthy coping strategies for dealing with change and stress, such as practicing mindfulness, exercise, hobbies, or even seeking professional help when necessary. By considering and acting on these decisions, our families can foster a supportive environment for navigating change and ensuring the mental well-being of all members.

What Results you can hope to see:

Growing up, I always envisioned my family as a big, happy unit, much like the family portrayed in the Bollywood movie K3G. I imagined a picture-perfect scene with all of us - parents, kids, and grandparents - together in a single frame, smiling and happy. However, I've come to realize that everyone's idea of a perfect family may be different, and that's okay. In the end, what matters is that we all find what works best for our own families and strive to create a supportive and loving environment for ourselves and our loved ones.

"You don't choose your family. They are God's gift to you, as you are to them."

- Desmond Tutu

By taking steps to navigate change as a family and support each other's mental health, we can hope to see several positive outcomes, including:

Stronger relationships: Building open and honest communication, establishing healthy boundaries, and supporting each other's emotional well-being leads to stronger and more meaningful relationships within the family.

Improved mental health: Developing coping strategies and finding ways to express emotions can help family members manage stress, reduce anxiety and depression, and promote overall mental health.

Increased resilience: By working together to navigate change and overcome challenges, family members develop resilience and the ability to handle future challenges more effectively.

Greater empathy: By understanding and respecting each other's needs and perspectives, family members develop greater empathy and emotional intelligence, leading to more harmonious relationships.

Enhanced sense of belonging: By sharing experiences and supporting each other, family members develop a stronger sense of belonging and connectedness, leading to greater overall satisfaction and happiness.

Ultimately, by prioritizing mental health and working together as a family, you can hope to see positive changes that lead to a happier, healthier, and more resilient family unit. By embracing the power of family bonds, we have the potential to inspire and create a positive ripple effect that extends far beyond our own lives.

#3
Loneliness in the Digital Age: How Technology Is Changing Our Sense of Connection and Isolation.

On the Outside

As social animals, loneliness is not natural to us. With fast-changing technology, we are more and more connected than ever before. But at the same time, the graph for depression and mental health issues due to loneliness has in fact gone up. As a social tribe, we are connected far, wide, and long digitally. These shallow connections often lack depth and emotional intimacy, leaving us feeling isolated despite the seemingly extensive networks we've built. In fact, more than 80% of my LinkedIn and Facebook connections consist of individuals I have never met or haven't spoken to in years.

There are several key factors at play in this phenomenon:

Superficial connections: Social media platforms encourage us to form a vast number of connections with people. However, these connections often lack the depth and emotional intimacy of face-to-face interactions. This leaves us feeling lonely and disconnected despite having a large number of "friends" or followers.

Comparison and envy: The curated lives displayed on social media creates a sense of inadequacy and envy, as users compare themselves to others' seemingly perfect lives. This leads to feelings of isolation and a lower sense of self-worth.

Reduced face-to-face interaction: As digital communication becomes the norm, people tend to spend less time engaging in face-to-face interactions, which are crucial for building strong relationships and fostering a sense of belonging. This leads to increased feelings of loneliness and isolation.

FOMO (Fear of Missing Out): The constant stream of updates on social media can create a sense of anxiety and FOMO, as we feel the need to keep up with others' lives and experiences. This further contributes to feelings of loneliness and isolation.

The impact of screen time: The increasing amount of time spent on screens negatively impacts our mental health, potentially exacerbating feelings of loneliness and isolation.

Overall, the digital age has had a complex impact on our sense of connection and isolation. While technology has made it easier than ever to stay in touch with others, it has also contributed to a growing sense of loneliness for many of us. To counteract these negative effects, it is important to be mindful of our technology use and prioritize meaningful, face-to-face interactions with others.

On the Inside

As technology keeps advancing, we see many new trends appearing. While it aims to save us time and effort by automating tasks, it also affects the way we communicate and maintain relationships with our friends and family. I remember when my father used to personally visit relatives and friends to invite them for important events like births, marriages, or funerals. Later, postcards and phone calls made it easier to save time and travel effort. Now, with social media and messaging apps like WhatsApp, we claim to be paperless, but in reality, we are becoming lazy and seeking convenience by trying to automate our relationships.

Our relentless pursuit of efficiency has transformed our relationships into transactions, as we trade meaningful exchanges for quick bursts of digital connection. While technology has undoubtedly enriched our lives in countless ways, it also created a distance between us, causing us to lose touch with the warmth and closeness of human connection.

The root causes of loneliness and isolation in the digital age can be attributed to several factors.

Some of the primary causes include:

The nature of online communication: Digital communication often lacks the nuances and non-verbal cues present in face-to-face interactions, which are essential for building deeper connections. Online communication can also be more prone to misunderstandings and misinterpretations.

The rise of social media: Social media platforms emphasize quantity over quality, encouraging users to accumulate more friends or followers. These connections are often superficial and do not provide the same emotional support as close relationships in the offline world.

The culture of comparison: Social media encourages us to compare ourselves to others, leading to feelings of inadequacy and envy. This constant comparison makes us feel more isolated and lonelier, as we perceive ourselves to be lacking in some way.

The decline of community and social structures: The digital age has seen a decline in traditional community structures and social institutions, such as religious groups, neighborhood associations, and clubs. These institutions have historically played a vital role in fostering connections and combating loneliness.

An increasingly individualistic society: Modern society places a high value on individual achievement and success, which leads to a focus on personal goals at the expense of social connections and relationships.

Digital distractions: The constant availability of digital distractions contribute to reduced opportunities for meaningful interactions and conversations, both online and offline.

Mental health issues: Mental health challenges, such as anxiety and depression, can be both a cause and a consequence of loneliness and isolation. The digital age may exacerbate these issues by contributing to feelings of inadequacy or by providing an unhealthy coping mechanism in the form of excessive screen time.

Digital technology didn't even exist three decades ago, and in the grand scheme of human history, this is a very short period of time. It's unclear what the long-term effects of rapidly changing technology will be on human mental health, and we don't yet know how we will be able to address these potential impacts.

In the near future, it's possible that we will have our own digital clone existing in a virtual metaverse. This digital clone will have its own personality, characteristics, and preferences that mimic our own, and it will be able to interact and communicate with other digital clones in the metaverse and beyond.

What Decisions do you need to consider?

It's difficult to resist the pull of technological advancements. As our friends, colleagues, and family members adopt new technologies, we feel a sense of FOMO (fear of missing out) and become increasingly drawn into the digital world. It's not realistic or desirable to reject technology entirely, as it has the potential to bring numerous benefits to our lives. However, what we do need is a sense of balance and intentionality in our technology use. We can use technology to discover new things, stay in touch with others, and access information, all while being mindful of the potential pitfalls.

The COVID-19 pandemic has accelerated the adoption of technology, making it an even more prominent part of our lives. As we navigate the post-COVID era, we need to develop hybrid approaches that allow us to combat loneliness and isolation in the digital age. With a balanced approach, we can harness the power of technology while still maintaining genuine connections and meaningful relationships with others.

We often focus on what we can add extra to improve our current situation, but sometimes success can come from the opposite approach.

It's not just about adding more, but also about eliminating and prioritizing what truly matters that can make all the difference.

Balance work-life and digital-life: Prioritize setting boundaries for both work and technology use to avoid burnout, and create space for personal connections and self-care.

Nurture authentic relationships: Focus on building and maintaining strong, genuine friendships and partnerships, both online and offline, rather than seeking validation through superficial social media connections.

Participate in interest-based groups and communities: Join clubs, sports teams, hobby groups, or professional organizations that provide opportunities to connect with like-minded individuals and form meaningful connections.

Utilize technology to enhance in-person experiences: Use digital tools to discover local events, activities, and meetups that facilitate face-to-face interactions, fostering a sense of belonging and connection in our community.

Develop a healthy relationship with social media: Limit time spent on social media platforms, and curate your feeds to include content that promotes positivity, self-acceptance, and realistic portrayals of life.

Embrace self-care and mental health support: Acknowledge the importance of mental health and wellbeing in combating loneliness, and utilize digital tools, such as mental health apps, online therapy, or support groups, to access resources and support when needed.

Network with intention: Engage in professional networking events and online platforms with a focus on building genuine, mutually beneficial connections, rather than simply accumulating contacts.

What Results you can hope to see:

In our fast-paced world, we often feel pressure to constantly add more to our lives - more commitments, more possessions, more experiences. However, sometimes the key to success and fulfillment lies not in what we can add, but in what we can eliminate and prioritize. By simplifying our lives, we can create space for what truly matters and achieve greater balance and contentment. Eliminating unnecessary distractions leads to increased productivity, mental clarity, and creativity. Prioritizing relationships and self-care lead to stronger connections and greater well-being. By taking a step back and focusing on what truly matters, we can create a life that is both meaningful and fulfilling.

By addressing loneliness and isolation in the digital age and implementing the suggested strategies, we can hope to see several positive results in our lives, including:

Improved mental well-being: Taking steps to combat loneliness and focusing on self-care can lead to better mental health, increased happiness, and a greater sense of overall well-being.

Stronger relationships: Fostering authentic connections and prioritizing meaningful interactions that lead to more fulfilling and supportive relationships with friends, family, and romantic partners.

Enhanced sense of belonging: Participating in interest-based groups, community events, and local activities to help us feel more connected and integrated into our community.

Greater work-life balance: Setting boundaries for work and technology use to lead to a healthier work-life balance, reducing stress and burnout while allowing more time for personal connections and self-care.

Reduced social comparison: By curating social media feeds and promoting realistic portrayals of life online, we can experience decreased feelings of envy and inadequacy, leading to improved self-esteem and self-acceptance.

Increased personal growth and self-awareness: By investing in self-reflection and personal development, we can gain a deeper understanding of ourselves, our needs, and our values, ultimately leading to a stronger sense of purpose and direction in life.

Positive online experiences: Encouraging empathy and kindness online results in more supportive and uplifting digital environments, fostering better connections and more satisfying online experiences.

More effective networking: By focusing on building genuine, mutually beneficial connections in professional and personal contexts, we can create more valuable and long-lasting relationships.

Reduced stigma surrounding loneliness and mental health: Open conversations about loneliness and mental health help normalize these topics, creating a more supportive and understanding culture both online and offline.

By addressing loneliness and isolation, we experience an increased sense of fulfillment and satisfaction in our personal and professional lives, leading to a more content and balanced life.

While the extent of these results will vary for each one of us, adopting the strategies will help in creating an environment where we can thrive, both in the digital realm and the real world.

#4

Moving On: The Psychological Impacts of Relocation and How to Cope

On the Outside

I first experienced the psychological impacts of relocation as a small kid. A childhood friend of mine, with whom I used to play after school and watch TV shows during summer breaks, suddenly disappeared from my life. As I grew older, I came to understand that my friend's family had to relocate frequently due to his father's career in the army.

I didn't fully understand the concept of relocation at the time, but the sudden gap created in my mind was undeniable. I missed my friend and our shared experiences, and it was difficult to come to terms with the fact that he was no longer a part of my daily life. It wasn't until years later, when I myself began relocating for studies, business, and jobs, that I truly understood the psychological impacts of relocation.

Relocation can be a challenging and stressful experience, particularly for those who are not accustomed to frequent moves. It is difficult to leave behind familiar surroundings, routines, and social connections, and to adapt to new environments, cultures, and expectations. This leads to feelings of loneliness, isolation, and anxiety, as well as a sense of loss and grief for what has been left behind.

On the Inside

Relocating has a range of psychological impacts, both for those who are actively relocating and for those who are left behind. From the perspective of those who are left behind, relocation leads to a sense of loss and emotional disconnect from friends and loved ones. This was my experience when my childhood friend relocated, and we lost touch as a result.

For those who are actively relocating, there are a number of psychological impacts that can arise. These include the disruption of social networks and familiar routines, which can be disorienting and lead to feelings of anxiety and stress. Additionally, there is a sense of uncertainty and instability about the future, particularly for older individuals who may have deep connections and attachments to their previous location.

In my own family, I witnessed the impact of relocation when my in-laws moved to be closer to us and our children. While the move was made to support us and strengthen family ties, they also experienced a sense of loss and disconnection from their familiar surroundings and social connections.

Relocating is complicated and has both practical and psychological impacts to consider.

Based on my own experiences, here are some of the causes of these impacts.

Loss of social connections: Relocation often means leaving behind friends, family, and social networks, which can lead to feelings of loneliness, isolation, and a sense of disconnection.

Disruption of familiar routines: Moving to a new location can disrupt familiar routines and activities, which can be disorienting and contribute to feelings of stress and anxiety.

Change in environment and culture: Adjusting to new cultural norms, social expectations, and physical surroundings, which is challenging and results in feelings of uncertainty and discomfort.

Uncertainty about the future: It creates feelings of uncertainty and instability about the future, particularly for those who are unsure about their job or housing situation.

Grief for what has been left behind: Relocation can also involve a sense of loss and grief for what has been left behind, including friends, family, and familiar surroundings.

These root causes can contribute to a range of psychological impacts, including anxiety, depression, stress, and a sense of disconnection. By recognizing and addressing these underlying issues, we can better cope with the psychological impacts of relocation and adapt to our new environment.

What Decisions do you need to consider?

Relocating can be a daunting prospect, whether it's for work, family, or personal reasons. As someone who has experienced relocation multiple times, I know firsthand the challenges and impacts that come with moving to a new location. It's a decision that requires careful consideration and planning, as well as a willingness to adapt to new surroundings, social networks, and cultural norms.

When considering a relocation, there are several decisions that need to be carefully considered in order to manage the practical and psychological impacts of such a move.

These decisions include:

The reason for relocation: Understanding why you are relocating and what you hope to achieve will help you make informed decisions about where to move, when to move, and how to prepare for the move. I left my hometown at the age of 16 for a bigger city to find independence and form my own identity.

The impact on social connections: Consider the impact of relocation on your social connections, both in terms of leaving behind existing connections and building new connections in the new location. This includes evaluating how relocation will affect our family, friends, and professional network.

The financial impact: Relocation is expensive, so it's important to consider the financial impact of the move, including the costs of housing, transportation, and other related expenses.

The impact on career and professional goals: Relocation has a significant implication for career and professional goals, including the availability of job opportunities, the cost of living, and the potential for professional development.

The impact on mental and emotional well-being: Relocation is stressful and disruptive, so it's important to consider the impact on our own mental and emotional well-being, as well as the well-being of family members who may be relocating with us.

By carefully considering these decisions and taking steps to manage the practical and psychological impacts of relocation, we can make informed choices that support our long-term goals and well-being.

What Results you can hope to see:

When I made the decision to relocate from a small town to a bigger city, I was excited for the opportunities it would bring for both personal and professional growth. However, I soon realized that relocating also came with significant challenges and emotional stress. The psychological impacts of relocation can range from feelings of isolation and disconnection to anxiety and uncertainty about the future.

I struggled without the right mindset and approach, but with time I could adapt and overcome and thrive in my new surroundings. By recognizing and addressing the root causes of these impacts and developing coping strategies to navigate the transition, I was able to manage the psychological impacts of relocation.

Through this experience, I have come to appreciate the many positive outcomes that can come from overcoming the psychological impacts of relocation. These outcomes include improved social connections, personal growth, expanded career opportunities, and enhanced mental and emotional well-being.

By taking steps to manage the psychological impacts of relocation, we can hope to see several positive results, including:

A sense of stability and security: By carefully considering the practical and emotional impacts of relocation and making informed decisions, we feel more secure and stable in our new location.

Improved social connections: While relocation can disrupt our existing social networks, it can also provide opportunities to build new connections and broaden one's social circle.

Personal growth and development: Relocating to a new location is a chance to try new things, explore new interests, and challenge oneself in new ways.

Professional opportunities: Relocation opens up new career opportunities and allows us to expand our professional networks.

Enhanced mental and emotional well-being: By taking steps to manage the psychological impacts of relocation, we can reduce stress and anxiety, improve our overall mental health, and enjoy a greater sense of fulfillment and satisfaction in our new location.

Overall, the results of relocation depend on the decisions and actions taken before, during, and after the move. By being mindful of the practical and emotional impacts of relocation and taking proactive steps to manage these impacts, we can successfully navigate the challenges of moving to a new location and enjoy the benefits that come with it.

#5

Relationship Changes and Mental Health: Navigating Breakups and Divorces

On the Outside

Breaking up in a relationship is never something we plan for or desire. When we enter a relationship with someone, we do so with the hope and expectation that it will last. However, as time goes on, the dynamics of relationships can change based on human expectations, and the ties of trust, loyalty, and communication that hold us together can begin to unravel. Whether it's with parents, spouse, children, friends, or family, the emotional toll of a breakup can be intense, and divorce can be an even more difficult form of separation. In India, the divorce rate is increasing every year, as modern youth are less willing to stay in a failed relationship compared to older generations who were more willing to compromise and adjust for decades.

The visible signs of relationship changes and mental health can manifest as:

Changes in behavior, such as increased irritability, mood swings, or withdrawing from social activities.

Physical symptoms, such as headaches, nausea, or a weakened immune system.

Changes in eating and sleeping habits, such as a loss of appetite or difficulty sleeping.

Substance abuse or addictive behavior, such as alcohol or drug abuse.

Self-destructive behavior, such as self-harm or suicidal thoughts.

Difficulty concentrating or focusing on tasks.

Decreased productivity and motivation.

Social withdrawal or isolation from friends and family.

Increased anxiety, depression, or stress levels.

Feelings of guilt, shame, or worthlessness.

Going through breakups and divorces can be really tough emotionally, as these relationship changes have a big impact on our mental health. It's important to take care of ourselves during this time, seeking support from loved ones or professionals who can help us navigate the difficult emotions and find our way to healing and building mental resilience.

On the Inside

As human beings, we all experience a wide range of emotions throughout our lives, and one of the most intense emotional experiences is the end of a romantic relationship. Whether it's a sudden breakup or a gradual separation, the end of a relationship can be a difficult and painful process that impacts our mental health and overall well-being. While some breakups may be initiated by external factors such as infidelity or physical distance, it's important to recognize that the real reason for a breakup is a personal one to the individuals involved. In order to move on and heal from a breakup, it's important to take the time to reflect on the underlying causes of the relationship's breakdown and find ways to address these issues in a healthy and constructive manner.

There are a variety of root causes that can lead to mental health problems following the breakdown of a relationship.

These include:

Loss of a sense of security and stability

A sense of betrayal or abandonment

Decreased self-esteem and feelings of inadequacy

Difficulty adjusting to changes in routine and lifestyle

Feelings of guilt or shame

Financial stress or instability

Legal complications and issues

Difficulty co-parenting and maintaining relationships with mutual friends and family

Trauma and triggers associated with the relationship

Mental health issues that were present before or developed as a result of the relationship.

What Decisions do you need to consider?

When navigating relationship changes and mental health, there are several decisions to consider to overcome the challenges and move towards healing and growth.

Some of these decisions may include:

Seeking professional help and support from a therapist, counselor, or support group

Identifying and processing emotions related to the breakup, such as sadness, anger, or guilt

Creating healthy boundaries with the ex-partner, including limiting or ending contact if necessary

Focusing on self-care and self-improvement, such as developing healthy habits, pursuing hobbies and interests, and setting goals for the future

Building and maintaining a support system of friends and family who can provide emotional support and encouragement

Reframing the breakup as an opportunity for personal growth and learning, rather than solely as a negative experience

Practicing forgiveness and letting go of resentment towards the ex-partner and oneself.

In the end, the decisions we make during this challenging time will depend on our individual circumstances and needs. It's crucial to prioritize self-care and reach out for support as we navigate through this phase of life. By taking care of ourselves and seeking guidance, we can find the strength to make choices that align with our well-being and forge a path towards a brighter future.

What Results you can hope to see:

Addressing the underlying causes of relationship changes and managing mental health challenges involves self-reflection, open communication, and sometimes seeking professional help. By understanding and addressing these factors, we can promote healthier relationship dynamics and enhance our mental well-being.

Taking proactive steps to navigate these changes can leads to positive outcomes:

Improved emotional well-being: Through the processing of emotions linked to the breakup and, if needed, seeking professional support, individuals can potentially witness a decrease in levels of depression, anxiety, and other adverse emotions.

Increased self-awareness and personal growth: By reflecting on the underlying causes of the relationship's breakdown and focusing on self-improvement, we can develop a greater sense of self-awareness and personal growth.

Strengthened relationships: During the healing process, we can enhance our social connections and find emotional support and encouragement by building and maintaining a support system of friends and family.

Greater resilience and adaptability: By reframing the breakup as an opportunity for growth and learning, developing greater resilience and adaptability in the face of future challenges can be made possible.

Enhanced overall well-being: Prioritizing self-care and making positive choices to support mental health leads to various benefits, including improved overall well-being, enhanced physical health, increased productivity, and a greater sense of purpose and meaning in life.

Ready starters for this Chapter to start implementing:

(Scan this QR for Mental Models, Links to Proven Frameworks and Excel templates to get started)

6

SPIRITUAL AND CHANGE

As a seeker on a spiritual path, I often ponder the difference between believing and seeking. To seek is to acknowledge that there is something greater than what we already know, something that we do not yet understand. It is to embrace the fact that we are ignorant to the essential nature of our own existence, to the source of creation and to our own identity.

Think of our mind as a container, like a cup or a pot. Believing is like filling our container with preconceived notions, like filling a cup with water. Once the cup is full, there is no more room for anything else. Seeking, on the other hand, is like starting with an empty cup and gradually filling it along the way.

When we are in a state of "I do not know," we are not in a position to fight anyone or anything. We are humble and open to the possibilities that lie ahead. It is this sincerity and openness that is the foundation of the spiritual process.

In my spiritual journey, I am learning to let go of my preconceived beliefs and notions, and acknowledge that I do not know everything. It is only when we admit to our ignorance that the possibility of knowing opens up. Beliefs, though they may seem comforting, limit our potential for growth and understanding.

To embark on this journey, we must turn inward. Inward is a dimensionless space that cannot be found on a map or compass. It is a space that can only be approached by someone who is straight within themselves, someone who is willing to be sincere and truthful with themselves.

Through mindfulness, gratitude, self-reflection, and the mind-body-spirit connection, we can navigate spiritual change and emerge stronger, wiser, and more grounded in our lives.

Some key topics on how changes impact our spiritual being

#1. Change Your Attitude, Change Your Life: The Power of Gratefulness in Transformation

#2. The Price of Not Being Present: How Lack of Mindfulness Impacts Your Life

#3. Stagnation: The Consequence of Ignoring the Spiritual and Scientific Sides of Change

#4. Achieving Holistic Transformation: The Mind-Body-Spirit Connection

#5. Spiritual Principles for Effective Leadership in Times of Change

#1
Change Your Attitude, Change Your Life: The Power of Gratefulness in Transformation

On the Outside

Looking back on my life, I can see that I used to be quick to judge and criticize others. Whether it was the close-mindedness of my small-town community, the stubbornness of the people in Chennai, or the laid-back approach to work in Kolkata, I always found fault in others without looking at my own thinking. But I failed to realize that this negativity was affecting my personal growth and well-being. We often overlook the little things that help us get through the day and take them for granted, leading to a toxic mindset.

Below are some of the experiences i had because of not changing my attitude towards gratitude:

Negative mindset: A negative mindset can have a detrimental impact on our lives. When we constantly blame others and focus on the negatives in our lives, we tend to adopt a negative mindset. I can recall times when I have gossiped or spread negativity in my neighborhood or workplace as a way of venting out my frustrations. This not only harms our relationships with others, but it also affects our work and overall well-being.

Lack of fulfillment: I realized that my life had become an accumulation of useless possessions, from excessive amounts of clothes to an ever-growing collection of gadgets and movies. The more I accumulated, the more I felt lost and unsure of what truly mattered in life. When we don't appreciate what we have, we constantly crave for more, leading to a sense of emptiness and lack of fulfillment.

Strained relationships: There was a time in my life when I failed to express gratitude towards the people in my life, including my parents, girlfriend, and some friends. This caused me to feel entitled and take them for granted, which led to a negative impact on my relationships with loved ones and colleagues. As a result, I experienced strain and tension in these relationships.

Poor mental health: Failing to appreciate the good things in our lives causes negative emotions and stress, which ultimately affects our mental health. It leads to issues such as anxiety, depression, and short temperedness. I have personally experienced this and still regret moments where I yelled at people in my personal and professional life.

Physical health problems: Our mental and physical health are deeply connected. Negative thoughts and emotions lead to chronic stress, which results in physical health problems such as high blood pressure, heart disease, and chronic pain. Additionally, negative emotions also cause poor posture, fatigue, and a weakened immune system.

On the Inside

The universe is vast and complex, with countless variables that could go wrong at any moment. The Earth's delicate ozone layer protects us from the harshness of space, while plants provide us with the oxygen we need to survive. Life itself is a fragile gift, and it's easy to take for granted the little things that make it all possible. The morning sunrise, a friendly smile from a stranger, or a birthday wish from a long-time old friend are all seemingly insignificant moments in our daily life.

When we fail to appreciate these moments, we miss out on the opportunity to experience the full richness of life. Not only that, but a lack of gratitude can actually hinder our ability to manifest more of what we want in life. When we focus solely on what we lack or what we want to change, we send a message to the universe that we are not content with what we have. This can make it more difficult to attract positive experiences and opportunities.

There can be several factors and underlying reasons on the inside that lead to a lack of gratitude, such as:

Self-centeredness: Being too self-centered causes us to overlook the good things that others do for us. When we are too focused on our own needs and desires, we become indifferent to the feelings and wants of others. We may not even realize how much they do for us, or how much we depend on them.

Comparison: Constantly comparing ourselves to others creates feelings of envy and jealousy, which makes it difficult to appreciate what we have. Our upbringing and family values play a significant role in shaping our tendency to compare ourselves to others.

Entitlement: When we feel entitled to things, we take them for granted and fail to appreciate them. This often leads to a lack of gratitude. I have observed this with some of my wealthy friends who seem to take things for granted and don't value them as much as they should.

Negativity bias: Our brains tend to fixate on negative events and experiences, making it difficult to appreciate the positive aspects of our lives. It's like a vortex that can suck us in and consume everything in its path, leaving us feeling drained and ungrateful.

Lack of mindfulness: When we are not mindful of the present moment, we may miss the good things happening around us. Our minds are constantly racing with thoughts of the past and future, and we may not see things as they are. It is important to be fully present and aware of our surroundings to appreciate the good things in life.

Stress and anxiety: When we are stressed or anxious, it is difficult to focus on the positive aspects of our lives. Our minds can get caught up in negative thoughts, making it hard to feel grateful for the good things around us...

Without gratitude as our attitude, true and sustained happiness is impossible. External factors alone cannot bring lasting happiness, and it is difficult to find things to be grateful for when we are unhappy with our lives.

What Decisions do you need to consider?

As we navigate through life, we are faced with a multitude of decisions that shape our experiences. It's easy to fall into the trap of complaining and focusing on the negatives, but it's important to recognize the good things that are happening in our lives. The fact that we are here reading this book is a testament to the positive aspects of our existence. By accepting our mistakes and taking ownership of our beliefs, we can cultivate a growth mindset and make decisions that align with our true identity.

Are you ready to overcome lack of gratitude? Here some of the decisions you can make today to start your journey towards a more grateful life:

Practice mindfulness: By being present and fully engaged in the present moment, we can develop an awareness and appreciation for the good things in our life. Start by taking a few minutes each day to sit quietly and focus on your breath.

Cultivate a gratitude journal: Each day, write down at least three things you are grateful for. This will help you shift your focus towards the positive aspects of your life and develop a habit of gratitude. It may sound simple, but it works!

Avoid comparison: Comparing yourself to others can lead to feelings of envy and dissatisfaction, making it difficult to appreciate what you have. Instead, focus on your own unique journey and progress. You are your own competition, be a better version every day, that's the path of growth and self-peace.

Practice empathy: By understanding and connecting with others, you can develop a greater appreciation for the good things in your own life. Try to put yourself in other people's shoes and understand their perspective.

Take action. Rather than simply feeling grateful, take action to show your appreciation for the good things in your life. This could mean expressing gratitude to others, volunteering, or simply taking care of your own well-being.

What Results you can hope to see:

I have come to understand the immense power of gratitude in shaping my experiences. It wasn't until I started to intentionally practice gratitude that I began to notice a significant shift in my perspective towards life. I realized that it's easy to take things for granted when we get caught up in the hustle and bustle of everyday life. Expressing gratitude is a beautiful way to show kindness and care towards others, which helps in building integrity, generosity, and closeness. Take a moment to reflect on the people who bring joy and support to your life, such as friends, family, mentors, or even colleagues who have been there for you.

We need to make a conscious decision to focus on the positive, exercise our gratitude muscle, and adopt a growth mindset to experience:

Improved mental health: Gratitude helps reduce stress and anxiety, leading to better overall mental health.

Stronger relationships: Practicing gratitude helps us appreciate the good things in your relationships, leading to deeper connections with loved ones.

Greater satisfaction: Focusing on what you have rather than what you lack can bring a sense of contentment and satisfaction to our life.

Better physical health: Studies have shown that gratitude leads to lower blood pressure, better sleep, and improved immune function. I have gained on my health parameters since I practiced this super power.

Increased resilience: By focusing on the good in your life, we can build resilience and better cope with difficult situations.

In the midst of our fast-paced lives, it's easy to get caught up in the struggles and setbacks we face. So why not give it a try? Keeping a gratitude journal is a simple practice that is easy to implement. It involves regularly writing down things you are grateful for, which can have a positive impact on our mindset and overall well-being.

Carve out a few minutes each week to reflect and express your gratitude. Your mental and emotional health will thank you for it.

#2

The Price of Not Being Present: How Lack of Mindfulness Impacts Your Life

On the Outside

As I watch my one-year-old son explore the world around him, I am struck by how present-focused he is. He's not worried about what happened yesterday or what will happen tomorrow; he's fully engaged in the moment, discovering the world around him with curiosity and wonder.

As we grow older, we tend to lose this present-focused mindset. Our minds become cluttered with worries, regrets, and distractions, and we forget to fully engage with the world around us. This lack of mindfulness has a profound impact on our lives, from missed opportunities and strained relationships to chronic stress and physical health problems.

Not practicing mindfulness has cost me dearly during my early days of career, its notable to share the below:

Poor communication skills: Have you ever been asked, "Are you listening to me?" This is because we may not be actively engaged and focused on what the other person is saying. This can lead to misunderstandings and miscommunication.

Difficulty focusing: Lack of mindfulness makes it difficult to concentrate on tasks, leading to decreased productivity and performance. High achievers strive to get into the "Flow state" and mindfulness is the key to it.

Impulsive behavior: People look at you as immature and you regret the consequences later on. Without being fully present, we may act impulsively without considering the consequences of our actions.

Poor decision making: I've made hasty decisions while multitasking and with a lot of confidence without checking the odds. When we are not fully present and aware, we tend to make poor decisions, which can lead to negative consequences.

Reduced empathy and compassion: Are you someone who frequently interrupts conversations with family or colleagues? Do you often find yourself more interested in making your point than listening to others? When we lack mindfulness, we struggle to connect with others and show empathy and understanding towards them.

Strained relationships: Lack of mindfulness can cause strain on our relationships, as we may appear inattentive and uninterested. When we are not fully present and engaged in our interactions, it leads to feelings of disconnection and puts a strain on our relationships with others.

It's easy to get caught up in the rush of everyday life and forget to be present in the moment. However, failing to be mindful has serious consequences, including increased stress and anxiety. When we're not fully engaged in the present, we're more likely to feel overwhelmed by the challenges we face. By practicing mindfulness, we learn to be more aware of our thoughts and emotions, which help us better manage stress and anxiety.

On the Inside

We live in an age of constant ding dang ping pong! The constant need to be connected and multitask makes it difficult to be fully present in the moment. Additionally, stress, anxiety, and the pressure to perform also contribute to a lack of mindfulness.

The reasons why we struggle with mindfulness differs from person to person, but there are some common factors that contribute to it, such as:

Distractions: It takes about 23 mins to regain focus once we are distracted! Living in a world full of distractions like social media, notifications, and endless to-do lists can make it difficult to focus on the present moment.

Multi-tasking: The No 1 killer of mindfulness in my experience. Trying to do too many things at once can lead to feelings of overwhelm and reduce our ability to be fully present.

Stress and anxiety: When we are stressed or anxious, it is difficult to focus on the present moment and instead, we are consumed with worries and negative thoughts.

Lack of self-awareness: If we lack self-awareness, we struggle to be fully present and engaged in our experiences. This is because without an understanding of our own thoughts, emotions, and physical sensations, we are in a state of self-denial and avoid taking responsibility for our mistakes.

Negative thought patterns: Negative thought patterns like self-criticism, rumination, and worry take us out of the present moment and lead to feelings of stress and anxiety.

By understanding the root causes of our lack of present-mindedness and working towards overcoming them through mindfulness and self-compassion, we cultivate a more present-focused and mindful approach to life.

What Decisions do you need to consider?

Just like small children being fully present and engaged in the moment, we too can learn to cultivate mindfulness and be fully present in our lives. It requires a conscious effort to let go of distractions and be fully engaged in the here and now. By doing so, we can experience a greater sense of peace, joy, and fulfillment in our lives.

Here are some definitive tips which worked wonderfully well for me:

Practice mindfulness meditation: Set aside time each day to sit quietly and focus on your breath, bringing your attention back to your breath whenever your mind wanders. This helps us to develop the ability to be present in the moment.

Disconnect from technology: Set aside time each day to disconnect from technology and focus on the present moment. This helps reduce distractions and allows us to be more fully engaged in your surroundings.

Cultivate self-awareness: Pay attention to the thoughts, feelings, and physical sensations throughout the day. This helps in becoming more self-aware and recognize when we are not fully present.

Engage in mindful activities: Engage in activities that require us to be fully present, such as drawing, yoga, exercising, or gardening. This helps in practically developing mindfulness skills.

Practice gratitude: Being grateful for the present moment helps us cultivate mindfulness and appreciation for the good things in your life. Take time each day to reflect on what you are grateful for.

What Results you can hope to see:

Being responsible for my own actions and positively looking at things helped me perceive the world with a different lens. I no longer spend time blaming the Gov, system or others. We got a gift and it's up to us how we lead our life.

Here are some results you can hope to see from cultivating mindfulness:

Improved mental health: Practicing mindfulness helps reduce stress, anxiety, and depression, leading to better overall mental health.

Stronger relationships: When we are fully present and engaged with others, we deepen our connections and build stronger relationships.

Increased focus and productivity: Mindfulness can help us stay focused and be more productive, leading to better performance at work or in other areas of our lives.

Greater sense of well-being: By focusing on the present moment and cultivating a sense of gratitude, we can experience a greater sense of contentment and well-being in our lives.

Improved physical health: Mindfulness has been shown to have a positive impact on physical health, such as reducing blood pressure and improving sleep.

When we actively cultivate mindfulness in our lives, we discover a more fulfilling and enjoyable existence. By being fully present and embracing gratitude, we can reduce stress and truly appreciate the little moments that bring us joy. This practice unlocks the true essence of a meaningful life, where peace, contentment, and gratitude become our constant companions.

#3
Stagnation: The Consequence of Ignoring the Spiritual and Scientific Sides of Change

On the Outside

In our modern world, we have access to unprecedented levels of comfort and luxury that our ancestors could only dream of. We have grown accustomed to instant gratification and convenience in every aspect of our lives, from the foods we eat to the temperature of our environment.

Throughout our evolution, our primitive brain developed as a survival mechanism to keep us alive in the moment. This "monkey brain" helped us respond to threats such as predators and danger in our environment, and it still plays a crucial role in our survival today.

However, the prefrontal cortex, located at the front of the brain, is responsible for executive functions such as planning, decision-making, and emotion regulation. When we fail to be mindful and regulate our emotions, we rely more heavily on our monkey brain than our prefrontal cortex.

I have realized that failing to adapt and evolve prevents us from living a fulfilling life. Although it may feel safer to stay the same, it can lead to stagnation and unfulfilled potential.

Some common reasons for this I have come across are:

- Societal pressures or expectations that discourage innovation, experimentation, or change
- Inadequate exposure to new ideas, cultures, or perspectives
- Negative influences from family, friends, or social circles that discourage personal growth or risk-taking

Limited job opportunities or financial resources that prevent individuals from pursuing new ventures or endeavors

Health or physical limitations that prevent us from taking risks or trying new things

Fear of failure or uncertainty, which creates a sense of comfort in maintaining the status quo

Overcommitment or a lack of time management skills that prevent us from pursuing new goals or opportunities

Geographical or cultural isolation that limits exposure to diverse perspectives or experiences

Traumatic life events or past experiences that have led to a sense of hopelessness or apathy.

On the Inside

We are wired to seek comfort and avoid discomfort. Our monkey brain that evolved to keep us safe in dangerous situations, can be easily manipulated by advertising, marketing, and other forms of media. These tactics are designed to appeal to our emotions and bypass our rational thought processes, and they can be indeed very effective.

As a result, we tend to prioritize comfort over logical analysis, allowing our emotional brain to guide our attitudes and behaviors. This leads to stagnation and a lack of personal growth, as we become complacent and resistant to change.

The reasons behind our tendency to prioritize comfort over logical analysis and allow our emotional brain to influence our attitudes and behaviors are diverse and intricate, and often overlooked from a spiritual and scientific perspective.

Some possible root causes include:

Evolutionary biology - Our brains evolved to prioritize survival, which can lead to an emphasis on avoiding discomfort and seeking out pleasurable experiences. If this is your default way of life, then personal growth is bound to be limited.

Cultural and societal norms - We live in a culture that values instant gratification and success, which leads to focusing on comfort and material possessions rather than personal growth. This is where spirituality and the seeker mindset set you apart from the rest.

Consumerism and advertising - Our society is inundated with advertising and marketing campaigns that promote products and services designed to provide comfort and instant gratification. The choices we take make or break us.

Personal fears and insecurities - When the mind is trapped in the past and fear of the future uncertainty, or discomfort, it prevents us from taking risks or pursuing new opportunities.

Lack of mindfulness and self-awareness - We may be unaware of our own thought patterns and emotional responses, and this lack of awareness makes it difficult to recognize when our emotional brain is guiding our decisions and behaviors.

Lack of access to resources and opportunities - Although with 4G and 5G Internet, this is changing fast, some sections of society may not have access to the free and open resources or opportunities they need to pursue personal growth or change, which contributes to feelings of stagnation and complacency.

Trauma or past experiences - Trauma or past negative experiences shape our worldview and influence our attitudes and behaviors, potentially leading to a focus on comfort and avoidance of discomfort.

It is important to recognize these tendencies and strive for balance between our emotional and rational selves. By embracing the spiritual and scientific sides of change, we can cultivate mindfulness and self-awareness, and develop the tools we need to navigate the challenges and opportunities that life presents us with.

What Decisions do you need to consider?

The path of transformation began for me when I realized that settling for the status quo was no longer an option. This realization may come from within, or be triggered by an external stimulus such as a life event, a friend, or a colleague. Personally, I found motivation in the works of Sadhguru, John Maxwell and Guy Kawasaki, but I soon realized that motivation alone was not enough to create lasting change.

In order to make meaningful progress towards the life I truly wanted, I needed to adopt new habits and mental models that would bring both short-term wow moments and long-term growth.

I found that the following mental models were particularly effective for me in overcoming stagnation by adopting spirituality backed by science:

Goal setting - prioritizing personal growth and development by setting SMART (specific, measurable, achievable, relevant, time-bound) goals and taking actionable steps towards achieving them. In an organization context, I found OKR goal setting very effective.

Mindfulness - practicing mindfulness and self-awareness to regulate emotions and make decisions with a clear and balanced perspective. Techniques such as deep breathing, meditation, and visualization helped me cultivate mindfulness.

Growth mindset - developing a growth mindset that embraces challenges, views failures as opportunities for learning, and prioritizes personal growth over comfort and security. "Atomic Habits" by James Clear helped me shape my new identity & mindset.

Deliberate practice - engaging in deliberate practice, which involves breaking down complex skills into smaller, manageable components and practicing them deliberately to achieve mastery until it's second nature to you, the hard work pays off.

Mental contrasting - imagine you are balancing between dreaming and facing reality. Nikola Tesla balanced his visionary ideas with the practical challenges of bringing them to life. It involves navigating between optimism and obstacles, it helps create a clear and actionable plan for reaching goals.

Social support - Having a circle of supportive friends and family who inspire personal growth and cultivate a positive outlook has been immensely beneficial to me. By prioritizing the quality of my relationships over their quantity, I have formed deeper connections...

Cognitive restructuring - The initial step towards eliminating feelings of stagnation or lack of progress is to recognize and challenge any limiting beliefs or negative self-talk. Subsequently, it's crucial to take massive action to overcome those beliefs.

Skill development - I conducted research and carefully selected one mentor for each skill I wished to improve upon. Then, I dedicated myself fully to learning everything that my mentor had to offer. This helped me arrive at a stage where I could self-correct.

Gratitude - Focusing on gratitude and positive aspects of life is a highly undervalued skill that requires consistent practice to truly appreciate its benefits. By cultivating gratitude and positivity, I could foster a sense of purpose and motivation in life.

The key to promoting personal growth is to embrace change and take calculated risks that push us beyond our comfort zones. Adopting a mental model of "calculated risk" can be immensely helpful in assessing the potential risks and benefits of a particular action before taking it. This approach is intentional, personalized, and can greatly increase the chances of success in improving one's skills and knowledge.

What Results you can hope to see:

After finding my purpose and setting goals, I found that I was able to sleep soundly and wake up energized without needing an alarm clock. I was even able to tackle the most challenging problems first thing in the morning. While your experience may be different, what's important is having the drive, energy, commitment, and discipline to strive towards self-improvement every day. By pushing your limits and gradually expanding your potential, you can achieve limitless growth and transform into a better version of yourself with each passing day.

By addressing the spiritual and scientific aspects of change, it is possible to overcome stagnation and experience a range of positive outcomes, including:

Renewed sense of purpose and meaning: By acknowledging and embracing the spiritual and scientific aspects of change, we can gain a deeper understanding of our purpose in life and find meaning in our experiences.

Increased creativity and innovation: Exploring the spiritual and scientific sides of change inspire new ideas and approaches, leading to greater creativity and innovation.

Improved problem-solving abilities: Integrating spiritual and scientific perspectives expand our problem-solving toolkit, enabling us to approach challenges from a more comprehensive and nuanced perspective.

Enhanced adaptability and resilience: Acknowledging the inevitability of change and actively engaging with it help us develop greater adaptability and resilience in the face of uncertainty and adversity.

Greater harmony and balance: Integrating spiritual and scientific perspectives can foster a greater sense of balance and harmony, promoting overall well-being and a more holistic approach to life.

Improved interpersonal relationships: Engaging with the spiritual and scientific sides of change led me to greater empathy and understanding of others, strengthening my interpersonal relationships and promoting cooperation and collaboration.

The journey of overcoming stagnation by embracing both the spiritual and scientific sides of change is a significant accomplishment, leading to personal growth and development. By expanding our knowledge, skills, and perspectives, we open ourselves up to new possibilities and experiences. This results in a greater sense of purpose, fulfillment, and self-awareness, as well as the ability to navigate challenges and obstacles with greater ease and confidence. Ultimately, leading to a more enriched and fulfilling life.

#4

Achieving Holistic Transformation: The Mind-Body-Spirit Connection

On the Outside

The essence of a gift is that it requires no investment on our part, which makes its value to us uncertain. Life on Earth is a precious gift. When given a gift, we can either cherish and nurture it, or simply take it for granted. In my twenties, my primary focus was on my outward appearance and the way I dressed. I cared deeply about how others perceived me. I ate whatever came my way, slept whenever I could, and took shortcuts in life.

It wasn't until I embarked on my startup journey that I realized the importance of cultivating the right mindset in order to persevere and make a significant impact. In the world of startups, ideas and founders face constant challenges and setbacks. I began to notice the positive effects and fleeting moments of happiness that came from working on my mind and body. Yet, there was still a lingering sense of emptiness and an unfulfilled void within me.

The Lack of mind-body-spirit connection can manifest in various external appearances and behaviors.

Here are some signs that may indicate a disconnection in one or more of these areas:

Emotional instability: This may manifest as frequent mood swings, irritability, excessive stress, anxiety, or depression. When the mind is not in harmony with the body and spirit, emotional wellbeing is negatively impacted.

Difficulty concentrating: A lack of connection in mind, body, and spirit result in an inability to focus, poor memory, and difficulty making decisions. This affected my work, relationships, and overall life satisfaction.

Poor physical health: This includes a lack of energy, frequent illnesses, weight gain or loss, poor sleep patterns, or chronic pain. Neglecting physical self-care is bound to throw mind-body-spirit connection out of balance.

Social withdrawal: In the absence of mind-body-spirit connection I had isolated

myself from friends and family, avoiding social events or losing interest in activities I once enjoyed.

Lack of motivation and purpose: There was a phase where I experienced feelings of apathy, a lack of motivation, and a sense of being lost or without purpose in life.

Compulsive behaviors: We may turn to unhealthy coping mechanisms like substance abuse, overeating, or other compulsive behaviors in an attempt to fill the void created by the lack of mind-body-spirit connection. I was guilty of over-eating as a means to numb my feelings and cope with daily stress.

Struggling relationships: A lack of balance in the mind-body-spirit connection results in difficulties in forming and maintaining healthy relationships. This manifests as frequent conflict, lack of communication, or an inability to connect on a deeper level with others.

Spiritual disconnection: Signs of spiritual disconnection include a lack of interest in exploring our spiritual beliefs, feeling disconnected from a higher power or sense of purpose, or a general sense of emptiness and dissatisfaction with life.

While these signs and appearances vary greatly from person to person and may not always indicate a lack of mind-body-spirit connection. However, if you notice several of these signs in yourself or someone you care about, it might be worth considering whether there is an imbalance that needs addressing.

On the Inside

As humans, we tend to have a natural desire to acquire material possessions and strive for status. Our culture and upbringing often promote materialism, leading us to constantly crave more. However, as I accumulated various belongings like clothes, watches, bags, cars, and bikes, I started feeling the burden of this pursuit weighing on my mind.

I found that while material possessions brought me temporary satisfaction, it wasn't long-lasting, and it didn't provide genuine fulfillment. As consumers, we prioritize convenience, comfort, and accessibility, trading our money for these luxuries. We work jobs to earn money and then spend it on lifestyle choices such as Netflix, social media, food delivery services, shopping, and entertainment. However, I realized that my journey as a creator and builder helped me understand the importance of integrating my mind, body, and spirit for true happiness and fulfillment.

There are several root causes for the lack of mind-body-spirit connection.

They can vary from person to person, but some common factors include:

Overemphasis on material success: Society often places a high value on material wealth and success, which leads us to prioritize these goals over our own well-being. This focus on external achievements leads to the neglect of inner growth and self-care.

High-stress lifestyles: In our city life, we lead a busy, high-pressure life that leaves little time for self-care and reflection. This constant state of stress and overstimulation makes it challenging to connect with our inner self and find balance among the mind, body, and spirit.

Lack of self-awareness: I was not aware of the importance of the mind-body-spirit connection, or how to foster this connection in our lives. This lack of self-awareness makes it difficult to prioritize self-care and personal growth.

Emotional and mental health issues: Unresolved emotional and mental health issues create barriers to achieving a healthy mind-body-spirit connection. Anxiety, depression, and trauma all interfere with our ability to connect with our inner self and maintain overall well-being.

Disconnection from nature and spirituality: Modern lifestyles often involve spending long hours indoors and focusing on technology, leading to a disconnection from the natural world and spiritual practices. This disconnection makes it more challenging to maintain a strong connection with the body and spirit.

Poor physical health: Neglecting physical health through poor nutrition, lack of exercise, and insufficient sleep impacts the overall mind-body-spirit connection. When the body is not well cared for, it is difficult to find balance and harmony in other aspects of life.

Lack of support and community: Having a supportive network of friends, family, and community is essential for maintaining a strong mind-body-spirit connection. When we lack this support, it is more challenging to prioritize self-care and personal growth.

Addressing these root causes and taking steps to create a more balanced, holistic lifestyle help us foster a stronger connection between our mind, body, and spirit. This involves setting aside time for self-care, seeking professional help for mental health concerns, engaging in spiritual practices, and cultivating supportive relationships.

What Decisions do you need to consider?

From a personal growth standpoint, a decision can't be objectively right or wrong, as long as you're able to accept and live with its consequences. Among the four quadrants of knowing, the most perilous one is the "I don't know I don't know" category. I was unaware that I lacked knowledge in the interconnectedness of mind-body-spirit, and it took me years to realize this. When I finally did, it was a humbling experience that made me realize how small and insignificant I am, and how little I know.

With this profound realization, I began to see life holistically, integrating the mind, body, and spirit. As a result, I started to experience moments of pure bliss.

When addressing a lack of mind-body-spirit connection, there are several decisions and considerations we need to make in order to improve our overall well-being:

Assess your current state: Awareness and being present-minded is the first step. Reflect on your physical, emotional, and spiritual health to determine which areas need attention. Be honest with yourself about your current lifestyle and habits.

Prioritize self-care: Make self-care a priority in your life. It's responsible, not selfish, to prioritize your own well-being. You can't help others if you're not okay. Prioritize physical health with exercise, nutrition, and sleep. Prioritize emotional and mental well-being with stress management, mindfulness, and personal growth.

Set realistic goals: Goals should be ambitious but achievable. Establish specific, achievable goals for each area of your life you want to improve. Break these goals down into smaller, manageable steps to help keep you motivated and on track.

Seek professional help if needed: If you are struggling to make progress on your own, consider seeking the help of a professional such as a therapist, counselor, personal trainer, or spiritual advisor to guide and support you through your journey.

Establish a support network: Share your goals and announce your intentions with friends, family, or like-minded individuals who will offer encouragement, advice, and accountability along the way.

Develop a daily routine: Small, seemingly inconsequential actions lead to significant results over time. Establish a daily routine that incorporates activities and practices that nurture your mind, body, and spirit. This includes meditation, exercise, journaling, or connecting with nature.

Be open to change: Be willing to reevaluate your goals and make adjustments as needed. Embrace the idea that personal growth and self-discovery are ongoing processes that require flexibility and adaptability.

Practice patience and self-compassion: Recognize that change takes time and that setbacks are a natural part of the process. Be gentle with yourself as you navigate your journey toward a more balanced mind-body-spirit connection.

Ultimately, the decisions you need to consider involve making a conscious commitment to prioritize your well-being and invest in your personal growth. By setting achievable goals, seeking support when needed, and maintaining a consistent practice, you can work towards strengthening your mind-body-spirit connection and enhancing your overall quality of life.

What Results you can hope to see:

By integrating the mind, body, and spirit, I have found a sense of ease in navigating difficult times. Rather than three separate areas, I see myself as one spiritual being. This approach has helped me learn from the past, stay present, and vividly visualize the future. As a result, I am better equipped to handle criticism, work towards my goals, incorporate feedback, and create value for my community.

Improving your mind-body-spirit connection can yield a range of positive outcomes, including:

Enhanced physical well-being: Just as a good software requires good hardware to run, a healthy body is necessary for a healthy mind. By fixing the basics i.e. prioritizing exercise, proper nutrition, and rest, you will experience increased energy levels, better sleep quality, and improved overall health.

Improved mental and emotional health: By managing stress, practicing mindfulness, and nurturing our emotional well-being, we find a reduction in anxiety and depression symptoms, increased focus and clarity, and better emotional resilience.

Greater self-awareness: As we engage in self-reflection and personal growth activities, we develop a deeper understanding of your own thoughts, emotions, and behaviors, enabling us to make more informed decisions and better cope with life's challenges.

Increased sense of inner peace and balance: By fostering a stronger mind-body-spirit connection, you will experience an increased sense of inner calm, harmony, and overall satisfaction with life.

Stronger relationships: As you become more in tune with yourself and your emotions, you will be better equipped to communicate effectively, empathize with others, and build deeper connections with the people in your life.

Heightened intuition and spiritual growth: By cultivating your spiritual side, you will experience a deeper sense of purpose and connection to something greater than yourself. This leads to an increased ability to trust your intuition and make decisions in line with your highest good.

Personal growth and self-discovery: As I made progress on my journey, I uncovered new interests, talents, and passions that contributed to my personal growth and self-discovery.

Prioritizing the development of a strong mind-body-spirit connection brings about a multitude of benefits. By becoming more resilient and adaptable, I could navigate life's challenges with greater ease and grace. Additionally, focusing on holistic self-care and personal growth led to improvements in various aspects of my well-being, including physical, mental, emotional, and spiritual health.

By cultivating a balanced and fulfilling life through this approach, you also can experience a greater sense of purpose and meaning in your daily existence. So, take the time to invest in yourself and your well-being, and reap the rewards of a more vibrant and thriving life.

#5

Spiritual Principles for Effective Leadership in Times of Change

On the Outside

During the initial phase of a startup, there is often an overwhelming sense of energy and conviction that failure is not an option, and the belief that anything can be accomplished. As a founder, you take on numerous roles – from recruitment and product development to sales and customer service – making the experience extremely fulfilling. However, soon it becomes evident that one person cannot do it all, and a strong team is essential for realizing the shared vision and achieving success.

Influencing and inspiring others is no small feat, and as a leader, I faced significant challenges. My shortcomings in understanding the nuances of leadership led to misunderstandings, and I was labeled as a tyrant, untrustworthy, and more. My rigid approach, impulsive decision-making, and tendency to induce stress in others only compounded the problem.

Lack of strong leadership principles during times of change can lead to various problems that impacts a business, the people working there, and the overall work atmosphere:

> **Employees leaving often**: Although hiring can do wonders for a business when done well, it remains one of the toughest challenges for many employers. However, when leaders fail to demonstrate care and understanding, employees may feel undervalued and choose to leave the company, resulting in a constant need to recruit new staff.
>
> **Low enthusiasm and involvement**: A strict and impulsive leadership style makes employees feel discouraged, leading to low enthusiasm, less involvement, and lower productivity.
>
> **Bad communication and teamwork**: Poor communication and teamwork results from trust issues with leadership, leading to reduced collaboration among colleagues. Additionally, conflicts and tense relationships with key people like investors, partners, and customers can arise from bad leadership practices.
>
> **Harm to the company's image**: Negative opinions about the leadership spread outside the company, possibly damaging the startup's image among potential customers, investors, and partners.
>
> **Less innovation & Limited growth**: As a business leader, I understood the importance of fostering a creative and supportive workplace environment. When employees feel stressed or unsupported,

their ability to generate new ideas and adapt to changing circumstances can be severely limited, which in turn can impede the growth of a business.

Poor decision-making: Making decisions too quickly without enough thought increases risk and potential failure. Difficulty adapting: Inflexible leadership can make it hard for the startup to adjust to quickly changing market conditions or take advantage of new opportunities.

As the leader of an organization, I recognize that financial stability and growth are critical to the success of the business. Losing employees frequently, reduced productivity, and limited innovation negatively impacts a startup's financial performance, making it difficult to achieve long-term growth and seize new opportunities.

On the Inside

Without any family history in business or a mentor, I had to navigate the challenges on my own.

As a leader, I was driven by a desire to prove myself and achieve success at all costs, without considering the well-being of my team or the long-term consequences of my actions. This led to a lack of compassion, empathy, and humility in my leadership style.

Without a foundation of spiritual principles, I was unable to build a supportive and collaborative workplace culture that fostered growth and innovation. Additionally, I lacked the necessary emotional intelligence to effectively manage relationships with team members, investors, and partners, leading to conflicts and tension.

Leadership challenges can arise due to a lack of spirituality in the mix.

Here are some reasons why not prioritizing spiritual principles in leadership can make it difficult to lead effectively:

Not caring enough about how others feel or showing kindness made it hard to work together as a team.

Only thinking about the short-term and not planning for the future led to problems.

Not creating a workplace where everyone supports each other caused issues and lower productivity.

Not being able to understand people's emotions and not managing relationships well caused conflicts and disagreements.

Only focusing on one's own success and not considering others in the mix led to issues in the company.

Not making ethical decisions and not being honest created problems.

Failing to be grateful and appreciative of others' hard work made people feel unimportant and unmotivated.

Being too proud and not willing to learn from others can make it difficult to improve as a leader.

Having trouble adapting to change or dealing with uncertainty caused problems for the company.

Not being able to inspire and motivate the team to work towards a common goal limited the success.

Prioritizing spiritual principles in leadership is crucial for effective leadership during times of change. Without a foundation of empathy, compassion, and humility, leaders may struggle to build a supportive and collaborative workplace culture, manage relationships effectively, and plan for the future.

What Decisions do you need to consider?

To become a more effective leader and overcome leadership challenges, it is important to recognize that change must first come from within. As John Maxwell wrote in his book "The 21 Irrefutable Laws of Leadership," leaders must focus on influencing others rather than just commanding them.

In order to influence others, leaders must first develop strong character and integrity, and demonstrate humility and a willingness to learn from others. They must also prioritize building strong relationships with team members and stakeholders, and communicate effectively to inspire and motivate them towards a shared vision. Additionally, leaders must develop a clear understanding of their strengths and weaknesses, and seek out guidance and support from mentors or coaches to help them grow and improve.

By focusing on the below key principles of leadership, we can become more effective in navigating the challenges of the modern business landscape and guiding their teams towards sustained success.

Prioritize self-reflection: I would rate this as the topmost quality. Leaders need to take the time to reflect on their values and beliefs, and identify areas where they may be lacking in spiritual principles. This can involve examining their actions, decisions, and interactions with team members.

Seek out mentors and guidance: The teachings of John Maxwell have had a significant impact on my leadership journey, and I continue to use his insights to this day. By learning from the experiences of others, leaders can fast-track their growth and development in this area.

Create a culture of compassion and gratitude: Leaders need to cultivate a workplace culture that values empathy, compassion, and gratitude. This involves acknowledging the hard work and contributions of team members, and encouraging collaboration and support among colleagues.

Communicate effectively: Effective communication is key to demonstrating spiritual principles in leadership. Leaders should strive to communicate with honesty, integrity, and transparency, and listen actively to the perspectives of others.

Embrace personal growth and development: Leaders should be committed to continuous personal growth and development, both in their personal and professional lives. This involves seeking out new knowledge and skills, and being open to feedback and constructive criticism.

Through deliberate actions and decisions, leaders can create a positive and collaborative work environment that fosters innovation, growth, and success. By leading with empathy, humility, and integrity, leaders can inspire their team members to work towards a common goal and achieve long-term success.

Ultimately, by prioritizing spiritual principles in leadership, leaders can create a workplace culture that values personal growth and development, fosters collaboration and support, and ultimately achieves success for the organization as a whole.

What Results you can hope to see:

Through my bootstrapped startup experience funded by dreams, compassion, and passion, I have realized the importance of spiritual principles in leadership. These principles are exhibited in the success of companies like Tata Group, Wipro, Zoho and Microsoft, who prioritize values such as empathy, integrity, humility, and compassion in their leadership.

As I worked with my team and stakeholders to create innovative solutions that would change the way the pharma and healthcare industry was run, I saw the impact of these principles firsthand. Our efforts resulted in saving countless hours for those involved in the profession, creating visibility for their leadership, and helping management make more informed decisions.

Although I regret refusing an offer from a top 3 VC firm, I view this as a valuable learning experience. I now understand that incorporating spiritual principles into my leadership style is key to creating a solid foundation for my business to grow and thrive.

These principles not only benefit the organization but also lead to a more positive and fulfilling workplace culture, which fosters innovation and success for all involved.

Improved workplace culture: Prioritizing empathy, integrity, humility, and compassion creates a more positive and fulfilling workplace culture, fostering innovation, growth, and success.

Better decision-making: Incorporating spiritual principles into leadership helps leaders make better decisions for the long-term growth and success of the organization.

Enhanced collaboration: By prioritizing empathy and humility, leaders create an environment that encourages collaboration, teamwork, and mutual support.

Increased trust: Spiritual principles such as honesty and transparency help leaders build trust with their team members, stakeholders, and customers.

Improved morale: A positive and collaborative workplace culture leads to improved morale and job satisfaction among team members.

Higher productivity: By fostering a positive workplace culture, improving collaboration, and making better decisions, leaders increase their productivity and drive the organization towards greater success.

Increased growth opportunities: By embracing spiritual principles in leadership, leaders are able to create a foundation for long-term growth and success, which in turn attract investors and open up new expansion opportunities.

By consistently working on these aspects we as leaders can build trust, foster collaboration, and make better decisions that benefit the long-term growth and success of our organization.

These outcomes have a ripple effect, leading to improved morale, increased productivity, and higher growth opportunities. By prioritizing spiritual principles in our leadership, we can create a positive and fulfilling workplace culture that attracts and retains top talent, while also driving innovation and success.

Ready starters for this Chapter to start implementing:

(Scan this QR for Mental Models, Links to Proven Frameworks and Excel templates to get started)

7

FAMILY AND CHANGE

As anyone else, I've experienced firsthand how changes can impact the dynamics and relationships within my own family. From moving to a new city, to adjusting to new family members through marriage or birth, to dealing with the challenges of aging parents, change is a constant factor in family life. Sometimes, it can be exciting as it brings positive outcomes, but other times it can be difficult and creates stress and tension within the family.

Families often encounter various changes, such as alterations in their dynamics, location, or financial situation. It's not uncommon for us to take our spouses or parents for granted, assuming they'll always be there for us. However, it's crucial to recognize that real relationships involve ongoing efforts to rediscover our partners and support them emotionally and intellectually, rather than treating marriage as a one-time event.

As time goes by, we tend to see our family members through the lens of their daily roles and responsibilities. I had attached them to certain mental structures, like parents as providers, children as recipients, siblings as supporters, and extended family as celebrators. However, this limited perspective can cause us to overlook their unique hobbies, skills, and personality traits. The environment can also play a significant role in shaping our perception of family members. When there is a change in the environment, it can provide an opportunity to see a different side of the person and break free from daily routines.

Family is built on the foundation of being present for each other, but sometimes this can lead to an imbalance in the supply and demand of support. For instance, when I was young, my mother was busy with her profession, and my grandmother stepped in to help raise me. Later in life, when my mother retired and had more time, I was busy with work and had less time to spend with her. Similarly, raising kids can sometimes lead to over-demanding situations where constant attention and care are needed, creating an imbalance in the family's support system.

By understanding the nature of change and its impact on families, we can learn to adapt, communicate, and support each other through these transitions.

Some key topics on how changes impact your family

#1. Balancing Tradition and Innovation in Modern Families

#2. Diversity and Inclusion in Family Relationships: Embracing Differences

#3. Parenting in the Digital Age: Challenges and Opportunities

#4. The Changing Role of Gender and Sexuality in Family Life

#5. Aging and Family Change: Supporting Elderly Family Members Through Transitions

#1
Balancing Tradition and Innovation in Modern Families

On the Outside

I remember my mother telling my child not to blow out the candles on his birthday cake. "In our tradition, we don't put out the Jeevan Deep," she explained. This experience made me reflect on the challenges that modern families face when trying to balance tradition and lifestyle. It's difficult to find a way to honor traditional values and practices while also adapting to modern life. Balancing tradition and innovation have become a challenge for families like ours, as we navigate the complexities of our cultural heritage and the demands of contemporary living.

But this blend of tradition and innovation creates conflicts within families. When family members have different ideas about what's important, it is challenging to find a balance. And when tradition clashes with innovation, it causes tension and misunderstandings.

Here are some of the external factors that contribute to the challenge of balancing tradition and innovation in modern families can include:

Societal pressure: Societal norms and expectations influence our families to prioritize traditional values over innovation. As social beings, we often feel the need to adjust to our society rather than go against it.

Globalization: Globalization has brought new ideas and practices to India, which sometimes conflict with our age-old traditional values. This makes it difficult for families to navigate the balance between tradition and innovation.

Changing economic conditions: Changes in economic conditions influence family dynamics and values. For example, in our family we need to adapt to new places, jobs, business and roles, which challenge traditional family values and practices.

Migration and urbanization: Migration and urbanization lead to changes in family structures and values. Families may need to adapt to new environments and cultural norms, which can create tension between tradition and innovation.

Technology: Technology has transformed many aspects of daily life, leading to new opportunities and challenges. Our families need to adapt to new technologies and their impact on social interactions, communication, and relationships, which can challenge traditional values and practices.

These external factors influence family dynamics and values, making it difficult to strike a balance between tradition and innovation. In many ways we have adopted western ways of life, technology, fashion, and food habits while still preserving our traditional values and practices like yoga, ayurveda, and other ancient wisdom. This has resulted in a unique cultural landscape that blends tradition and innovation.

On the Inside

In India, tradition and cultural practices are deeply ingrained in family life, while at the same time, the country is rapidly changing and modernizing, bringing with it new opportunities and belief systems. India is a country that values its rich history as well as its progress in modern times. This has resulted in an ongoing challenge for many families to balance tradition and innovation, leading to both internal and external impacts on family dynamics.

Balancing tradition and innovation are challenging for modern families because these two forces appear to be contradictory. Traditions often represent a deep connection to cultural heritage, history, and values that have been passed down through generations. They provide a sense of continuity, belonging, and stability. On the other hand, innovation represents progress, change, and adaptation to new circumstances. It enables us to explore new ideas, challenge old ways of thinking, and create new possibilities.

The root causes that contribute to the challenge of balancing tradition and innovation in modern families I have witnessed are due to:

Personal values and beliefs: Each family member may have different personal values and beliefs, which can create conflicts when trying to balance tradition and innovation. While my parents place a great deal of importance on traditional religious practices, I prioritize individual freedom, independence, and self-discovery.

Emotional attachment to tradition: We see in our families having emotional attachments to certain traditions, which make it difficult to let go of them, even if they conflict with innovation. This leads to resistance to change and tension within the family.

Fear of losing identity: I have experienced my family members fearing that adopting new practices will lead to the loss of our cultural identity. This fear makes it challenging to embrace innovation and can create tension within the family.

Generational differences: Different generations may have different perspectives on tradition and innovation, which create conflicts within the family. It is often seen that older family members are more attached to traditions, while younger members may be more open to innovation.

Parental authority: Parents may have different expectations for their children in terms of adhering to traditional values and practices. This can create tension between parents and children, and can make it challenging for children to balance tradition and innovation.

Lack of understanding: Family members may have a lack of understanding or knowledge about the benefits and importance of innovation. This makes it challenging to embrace new practices and create tension within the family.

The deep root causes of these internal factors can be traced back to cultural, historical, and social factors that shape family dynamics and values. It takes considerable time and effort for families to navigate these internal factors and find a balance between tradition and innovation that works for everyone.

What Decisions do you need to consider?

As someone who travels for work between the UK and Asia, I've had the opportunity to witness firsthand how families from different cultures - including my partners, colleagues, and their families - are grappling with the challenge of balancing tradition and innovation. It's a challenge that's not limited to any one culture or country, as families all over the world try to integrate new ideas and values while still respecting their cultural traditions and heritage.

As the world becomes more interconnected through advances in telecommunication, road, and air infrastructure, we are presented with both opportunities and challenges. We need to find a way to balance these two opposing forces so that we can progress, grow, and nurture our families. By doing so, we can create a positive and fulfilling family experience that prepares us and our loved ones for success in a rapidly evolving world.

When trying to balance tradition and innovation in modern families, there are several decisions that family members may need to consider.

These decisions may include:

Prioritizing family values - Try to find the non-negotiables. Family members need to consider which values are most important to the family and how they can balance tradition and innovation while still upholding these values.

Evaluate the benefits and drawbacks - Family members need to evaluate the benefits and drawbacks of embracing tradition or innovation in various areas of their lives, such as education, careers, or social relationships.

Communicating openly & effectively - Family members need to consider how to communicate their perspectives and concerns effectively to each other, in order to reach a common understanding and find a balance that works for everyone.

Seeking support proactively - A counselor or mediator can help family members understand each other's perspectives and work through any conflicts or challenges that arise. They can also provide tools and strategies for managing internal factors like personal values and beliefs, emotional attachment to tradition, and generational differences.

Compromising is not a sign of weakness - Family members may need to consider compromising and finding common ground between traditional and innovative ideas, in order to maintain a cohesive and harmonious family dynamic.

Navigating generational differences - Family members can work together to navigate generational differences and find a balance that respects everyone's values and beliefs. By acknowledging differences, listening and communicating effectively, finding common ground, and being flexible and open-minded, we can create a supportive and harmonious environment that embraces both tradition and innovation.

It is possible to honor cultural heritage while embracing the benefits of innovation and progress. Families should be willing to embrace change and explore new ideas, technologies, and routines to adapt to changing times. By doing so, they can create a supportive and healthy family dynamic that values both tradition and innovation.

What Results you can hope to see:

It is important to remember that finding a balance between tradition and innovation is an ongoing process that requires open communication, compromise, and mutual understanding. Families should continue to re-evaluate their traditions and practices to ensure they remain relevant and meaningful. By working together, families can navigate the challenges of balancing tradition and innovation in modern times and create a positive and fulfilling family experience for generations to come.

By applying the strategies and insights provided in this book, families can hope to see several positive results.

These can include:

Strengthened family bonds: By engaging in open communication, families can create a stronger sense of understanding and respect for each other's perspectives. This can lead to a more supportive and cohesive family dynamic.

Enhanced cultural appreciation: Families can develop a deeper appreciation for their cultural heritage by re-evaluating traditions and understanding their significance.

Improved adaptability: By embracing change and innovation, families can become more adaptable to new situations and challenges.

Increased creativity: Families can tap into their creativity and find new ways to approach challenges and solve problems by exploring new ideas and practices.

Overall growth and progress: By finding a balance between tradition and innovation, families can create a positive and constructive environment for growth and progress, both individually and as a family.

When the balance between Tradition and Innovation is made, our families will be able to maintain a strong bond while still embracing change and progress, and that they will be able to create a supportive and harmonious environment that reflects our unique cultural landscape. By working together, we can navigate the challenges of modern times and create a fulfilling and meaningful family experience that values both the past and the future.

#2

Diversity and Inclusion in starting new Family: Embracing Differences

On the Outside

When I was in 3rd grade, my friends and I would form teams during our summer break and play various silly games. Some of my friends lived in small huts and were sons and daughters of daily wage workers. However, my mother used to ask me to stay away from them. As a kid, I didn't understand the real reasons, and I used to fight and argue with my mother, as she looked down upon my friends and judged them.

As I look back on my childhood, I realize that my mother's behavior towards my friends from certain families was due to caste-based discrimination. Sadly, this was not the only instance of discrimination that I observed as I grew up. In fact, I witnessed more examples of this type of behavior in society when it came to marriage. It became clear to me that discrimination based on caste, race, ethnicity, culture, and religion are some of the pressing issues that can arise when starting a new family, causing significant challenges and complications.

Several external factors can contribute to a lack of diversity and inclusion in starting a new family.

Some of them are:

> **Social norms and expectations**: Society often expects families to conform to traditional cultural norms and values, which leads to exclusion of those who don't fit the mold.
>
> **Historical factors**: The history of a particular community or society influences the way families perceive and treat people from different backgrounds.
>
> **Geographic location**: The region in which a family resides influences their exposure to diverse cultures and traditions.
>
> **Education and socio-economic status**: Education and socio-economic status play a significant role in shaping a person's attitudes and beliefs towards diversity and inclusion.
>
> **Political climate**: The political climate of a country or region impacts how families perceive and treat people from different backgrounds.

Recognizing and understanding the external factors that contribute to a lack of diversity and inclusion in starting a new family is crucial for creating an inclusive and welcoming family environment. Taking steps to address these external factors help break down barriers to acceptance and understanding, promoting diversity and inclusion in family relationships.

On the Inside

When families don't accept and welcome different people, some individuals may be left out or treated unfairly. Society's beliefs and behaviors can cause this, which can come from things like our culture, history, and education. Some religious rules, like caste systems, can also contribute to this problem, as they only allow people to marry within their own group.

Furthermore, even religious teachings can support such exclusionary practices. For example, caste systems dictate who can marry whom, with members of each caste following restrictions to maintain racial purity.

The absence of diversity and inclusion in new families can be attributed to multiple root causes:

- Societal attitudes and beliefs
- Cultural norms and expectations
- Historical factors and social conditioning
- Religious doctrines and traditions
- Fear and prejudice towards people who are different
- Lack of exposure and education on diversity and inclusion
- Ignorance and misinformation
- Stereotyping and discrimination based on race, ethnicity, culture, religion, and caste
- Power imbalances and systemic oppression
- Lack of representation and inclusion in media and leadership positions.

What Decisions do you need to consider?

Education has helped us break free from the narrow-minded thinking that prioritizes caste, race, ethnicity, culture, and religion when it comes to starting a new family. When my partner and I fell in love, it was simply because we enjoyed spending time together, even doing the most mundane activities. In the end, what matters most is love, affection, and trust, rather than outdated doctrines and practices.

In promoting diversity and inclusion within our family, we are wholeheartedly ready to embrace whomever our child chooses as their life partner in the future. We firmly believe in fostering an open society that values diverse perspectives, ideas, and equal opportunities for everyone.

To promote diversity and inclusion in family relationships, family members may need to consider several decisions, such as:

Recognizing biases: Families need to recognize their own biases and assumptions that limit their understanding of diverse perspectives.

Learning about different cultures: Families should educate themselves about different cultures and traditions, and be open to learning about new experiences and perspectives. For me traveling helped break a lot of my limiting beliefs.

Encouraging open communication: Families should encourage open and honest communication, and be willing to listen to each other's perspectives and experiences.

Creating an inclusive environment: Families should create an inclusive environment by actively seeking out diverse perspectives and experiences, and by avoiding exclusionary practices.

Celebrating differences: Families should celebrate diversity by embracing differences in backgrounds, experiences, and perspectives, and by valuing and respecting the unique qualities of each family member.

By considering these decisions, families can promote a more inclusive and accepting family environment that values diversity and strengthens family bonds. When we promote love, respect, and equality, we hope to inspire other families to join us in fostering a world where everyone feels accepted and celebrated for their unique selves.

What Results you can hope to see:

Diversity and inclusion in family relationships are essential for building strong and supportive family bonds. Every family is unique, with different backgrounds, experiences, and perspectives. Embracing this diversity and creating an inclusive family environment leads to greater empathy, understanding, and innovation. We explore the importance of diversity and inclusion in family relationships, the challenges that families may face, and the strategies that families can use to promote a more inclusive and accepting family environment.

By promoting diversity and inclusion in family relationships, families can hope to see several positive results, including:

- **Increased empathy and understanding**: By learning about different cultures and perspectives, family members develop greater empathy and understanding towards each other, leading to stronger family bonds.
- **Strengthened family relationships**: Families that value and celebrate diversity are likely to have stronger and more supportive family relationships.
- **Greater creativity and innovation**: Encouraging diverse perspectives and experiences can lead to greater creativity and innovation in problem-solving and decision-making.
- **Improved mental health**: An inclusive and accepting family environment can improve the mental health of family members, creating a more positive and supportive atmosphere.
- **Positive impact on society**: By promoting diversity and inclusion within families, families can create a positive impact on society, promoting acceptance and understanding of different cultures and backgrounds.

Prioritizing diversity and inclusion in family relationships, leads to a more positive, supportive, and fulfilling family experience for all members. By recognizing and addressing the root causes of the lack of diversity and inclusion in family relationships, families can create a more accepting and inclusive environment that values and celebrates differences.

By making the decision to prioritize diversity and inclusion, families can hope to see several positive results, including strengthened family bonds, greater creativity and innovation, and an improved mental health for all members. Ultimately, by promoting diversity and inclusion in family relationships, families can create a positive impact on society, promoting acceptance and understanding of different cultures and backgrounds.

#3
Parenting in the Digital Age: Challenges and Opportunities

On the Outside

During our family gatherings, we often discuss the challenges that our parents and grandparents faced while raising us. We acknowledge the sacrifices, time, love, attention, and care they invested in us, which we can never fully repay. While times have changed, the core values of love, care, and affection with which we raise our children remain the same. However, parenting in the digital age has become more complex due to various external factors.

Factors such as the constant evolution of technology, the increasing use of social media, the amount of time children spend on screens, changes in cultural norms and values related to parenting, and economic factors can create new challenges for parents. These factors can have an impact on the health and development of their children, making it crucial for parents to adapt and learn how to navigate these challenges.

External factors that contribute to the challenges of parenting in the digital age include:

Technology: The constant evolution of technology and the increasing pervasiveness of digital devices in everyday life have created new challenges for parents. Children are exposed to a wide range of digital media and online content, which can be both educational and entertaining, but can also be harmful or inappropriate.

Social media: Social media platforms have created new challenges for parents, including cyberbullying, the pressure to present a perfect image of their family, and the potential for children to be exposed to inappropriate or harmful content.

Screen time: The amount of time that children spend in front of screens has increased dramatically in recent years, which can have negative impacts on their health and development.

Cultural norms & pressure to keep up: Cultural norms and values related to parenting have changed over time, and parents may feel pressure to conform to new standards of parenting in the digital age. There may be pressure on parents to keep up with the latest technology trends and provide their children with access to digital devices and online resources, which can create additional stress and financial burdens.

Fear of missing out: Parents may fear that their children will miss out on opportunities or fall behind their peers if they are not exposed to the latest technology and online resources.

Economic factors: Economic factors, such as the cost of digital devices and internet access, can create barriers for parents who want to provide their children with access to technology but cannot afford it. This can create disparities in access to digital media and online resources, which can have long-term impacts on children's education and opportunities.

On the Inside

In today's world, technology has advanced at an incredible pace, leading to significant changes in the way we live. With the rise of smart cities, implementation of 5G networks and AI systems we have access to a wealth of information and convenience that was unimaginable in the past. In addition, the emergence of technologies such as the metaverse and augmented reality is set to revolutionize our lives even further.

However, the rapid growth of technology has also introduced new challenges, particularly for parents raising children in the digital age. The constant exposure to digital media and online content have both positive and negative effects on children's growth and well-being.

The root causes of the challenges and opportunities of parenting in the digital age include:

Advancements in technology: Technological advancements have made digital devices and the internet more accessible than ever before. This has resulted in children being exposed to a wide range of online content and media, which can be both beneficial and harmful.

Lifestyle changes: Modern-day lifestyles, particularly in urban areas, have become faster-more paced and demanding. This has created new challenges for parents who need to balance their work, family and personal life, while also monitoring and managing their children's use of technology.

Cultural shifts: Cultural values and norms have evolved over time, including changes in how parents approach discipline, education, and family dynamics. These changes can impact how parents navigate the use of technology in their children's lives.

Economic factors: Economic factors, such as the cost of technology and access to the internet, can create disparities in access to digital media and online resources. This can have long-term impacts on children's education and opportunities.

Opportunities for learning and growth: The digital age also presents new opportunities for children to learn and grow, including access to educational resources and platforms, networking and communication tools, and exposure to diverse perspectives and experiences.

Overall, parenting in the digital age requires parents to navigate a complex landscape of technological advancements, cultural shifts, and economic factors, while also leveraging the opportunities that technology presents for their children's learning and growth.

What Decisions do you need to consider?

As a parent in the digital age, finding the right balance between independence and accountability for our children has been a crucial decision. In our family, we believe in the "Trust but verify" rule; giving our children the freedom to grow and explore while ensuring their safety.

To achieve this, we prioritize open communication channels and encourage our children to talk to us openly and without fear about any issues or concerns they may have. By doing so, we can provide guidance and support to help them navigate the challenges that come with living in a world increasingly shaped by technology.

As parents, we've found some strategies useful in promoting independence, accountability, and safety while raising responsible and independent children in the digital age.

To overcome parenting challenges in the digital age, there are several decisions that parents can consider:

Establish clear rules and boundaries: Setting clear rules and boundaries around the use of digital devices and the internet help to minimize potential risks and create a healthier balance between screen time and other activities.

Monitor children's digital activity: Monitoring children's digital activity helps parents to identify potential risks, such as cyberbullying or exposure to inappropriate content, and take appropriate action.

Encourage open communication: Encouraging open communication with children can help parents to understand their children's online behavior and experiences, and provide guidance and support as needed.

Educate children about responsible digital citizenship: Teaching children about responsible digital citizenship, including online safety and privacy, can help them to make informed decisions and protect themselves online.

Model healthy digital behavior: Children learn by example. Parents can model healthy digital behavior by limiting their own screen time, being mindful of their online presence, and demonstrating responsible digital citizenship.

Use technology to enhance learning and growth: The digital age also presents opportunities for children to learn and grow, and parents can consider using technology to enhance their children's education and personal development.

By considering these decisions, parents can navigate the challenges of parenting in the digital age and create a safe and healthy environment for their children.

What Results you can hope to see:

As parents, we need to strike a balance between granting our children independence while holding them accountable for their actions. In today's digital era, it is crucial to establish open communication with our children and provide a safe environment for them to learn and develop.

By making mindful decisions in raising responsible and independent children in the digital age, we can anticipate seeing several positive outcomes.

Some of these results may include:

Stronger family relationships: By maintaining open communication channels and fostering a positive and supportive family dynamic, parents build stronger relationships with their children.

Increased independence and accountability: By giving children the freedom to explore and grow within a regulated and safe environment, parents help them develop independence and accountability.

Improved safety: By being proactive in promoting safety and responsible behavior online, parents help protect their children from potential dangers.

Greater confidence and resilience: By providing guidance and support as children navigate the challenges of the digital world, parents help them develop greater confidence and resilience.

Positive impact on society: By raising responsible and independent children who understand the importance of safety and accountability, parents help create a positive impact on society as a whole.

Parents can ensure a positive and fulfilling family experience for their children in the digital age by considering the decisions involved in raising them. By following the rule of "Trust but verify," parents can help their children develop independence and accountability while also keeping them safe online. These efforts result in stronger family relationships, increased confidence and resilience, and a positive impact on society.

#4
The Changing Role of Gender in Family Life

On the Outside

Growing up in my family, I had the privilege of witnessing the impressive achievements of several incredible women. My illiterate grandmother, for instance, was able to successfully manage a cow milk selling business, while my mother slogged hard to fund her own education and later retired as a school head-mistress. Today, my wife is a busy mother of two children and a successful banker.

However, despite the prevalence of strong and successful women in my family, gender-based roles and responsibilities still exist in our society due to societal expectations and family customs. Typically, women are expected to take care of household chores while men are expected to go out for work or business, as is common in many societies.

The lack of changing roles of gender in family life have several negative consequences.

Some of these include:

> **Gender Inequality**: When traditional gender roles are strictly adhered to, women are often relegated to being the primary caregivers and homemakers, while men are expected to be the primary breadwinners. This leads to gender inequality, where women are undervalued and not given the same opportunities as men to pursue their interests and careers.

Limited Family Structures: Traditional gender roles also limit the types of family structures that are considered acceptable. For example, same-sex couples and single parents may be stigmatized or excluded from certain social and cultural norms.

Lack of Flexibility: When both parents work outside the home, but only one is expected to take care of the children and the home, it can put undue pressure and stress on that parent.

Negative Impact on Children: Traditional gender roles also hurt children. Children may grow up with limited role models and ideas about what it means to be a man or a woman. They may also experience gender-based discrimination, leading to low self-esteem and other emotional issues.

According to a research by the World Health Organization has found that gender stereotypes have negative impacts on children, leading to low self-esteem, body image issues, and mental health problems. Children who grow up in families where traditional gender roles are strictly adhered to are also more likely to perpetuate these stereotypes, perpetuating the cycle of gender inequality and discrimination.

On the Inside

As society continues to evolve and progress, traditional gender roles and family structures are being challenged and redefined. Meghalaya, a state located in the northeast part of India, has a unique approach to gender roles. The Khasi families in this state have a matrilineal system where women play a dominant role in the family, managing finances and running the household, while men take care of the children and perform domestic tasks.

But this is not true for the majority of India, the root causes of traditional gender roles still existing in many societies are complex and multifaceted, involving gender stereotypes, historical and cultural biases, systemic discrimination, and societal expectations.

The root causes for this are many and I have come to observe the below:

Lack of education and awareness: A lack of education and awareness about the negative impacts of traditional gender roles perpetuate the cycle of gender inequality, leading to limited opportunities and negative impacts on women and our society.

Historical and cultural biases: Women have historically been excluded from education and employment opportunities, resulting in a lack of representation of women in leadership positions, perpetuating the cycle of gender inequality. There is a lot of catching up to do still to come to a fair ratio of equality.

Gender stereotypes: Reinforced through media, web-series, advertising, and socialization, gender stereotypes dictate traditional gender roles, where women are expected to be caregivers and homemakers while men are expected to be breadwinners and providers.

Economic factors: The gender pay gap and lack of affordable childcare reinforce traditional gender roles, where women may be forced to prioritize childcare over pursuing their careers.

Societal expectations and pressures: Pressures to conform to traditional gender roles create a cycle of self-fulfilling prophecy, where individuals feel compelled to adhere to these roles even if they do not align with their personal aspirations or abilities.

What Decisions do you need to consider?

It is important to question whether gender roles in the family are an either-or situation between males and females or if there should be a balance and harmony between both genders. The consequences of how gender roles are defined and implemented have far-reaching impacts on individuals, families, and society as a whole. As we continue to explore and evolve, it is crucial to strive towards creating a more equitable and inclusive society where everyone is able to reach their full potential, regardless of their gender.

At an individual level, there are several decisions that we can consider to help create a more equitable and inclusive society:

Challenge your own biases and assumptions: Hear yourself, take time to reflect on your own biases and assumptions about gender roles and work to challenge them. This can involve examining the way you communicate with and treat individuals of different genders, as well as exploring new perspectives and experiences.

Encourage open communication and dialogue: Create an environment where open communication and dialogue about gender roles and stereotypes is encouraged. This involves having honest conversations with friends, family, and colleagues about their perspectives and experiences.

Support gender equality initiatives: Support initiatives and organizations that promote gender equality and work to break down traditional gender roles. This involves volunteering, donating, or participating in activism efforts.

Be a role model: Serve as a role model for those around you by challenging traditional gender roles and stereotypes. This involves leading by example in your personal and professional life and supporting those who are working to create a more equitable and inclusive society.

By making these decisions at an individual level, we can all work towards creating a society that is more equitable and inclusive, where everyone has equal opportunities to pursue their dreams and reach their full potential, regardless of their gender. This means creating an environment where the best ideas, execution, and causes are able to materialize regardless of who they came from.

What Results you can hope to see:

Growing up, Moon always knew that she was different from her peers. She loved playing sports and exploring the outdoors, while many of the girls in her class preferred to play with dolls and dress up. However, she quickly learned that these interests were not seen as "appropriate" for a girl and often faced teasing and bullying from her classmates.

As she got older and more aware of the gender stereotypes and expectations that were placed on her and other girls, she became an advocate for gender equality and to work towards creating a more equitable and inclusive society.

Our micro actions have a far-reaching impact on fostering a fair and inclusive society.

Here are some of the positive outcomes we can expect to witness as a result:

- **Increased diversity and innovation**: By breaking down traditional gender roles and promoting gender equality, we can increase diversity and innovation in all aspects of society. This can lead to new ideas, perspectives, and approaches that can help solve complex problems and drive progress.
- **Improved mental health and well-being**: When we are able to pursue our interests and passions without being constrained by gender stereotypes and roles, we experience improved mental health and well-being. This leads to greater happiness and fulfillment in both personal and professional life.
- **Increased productivity and economic growth**: When everyone has equal opportunities to pursue their careers and reach their full potential, it leads to increased productivity and economic growth. This benefits individuals, families, and society as a whole.
- **Greater social and cultural acceptance**: By promoting gender equality and breaking down traditional gender roles, we create a more accepting and inclusive society. This leads to greater social and cultural acceptance of individuals of all genders and backgrounds.

Moon is my wife's nickname, and she has been an activist for women rights and equality in the workplace and society. She has seen how increased diversity, innovation, and social acceptance leads to greater happiness, fulfillment, and economic growth for everyone.

As we continue to evolve and progress as a society, it is important to prioritize gender equality and work towards creating a more equitable and inclusive world. By doing so, we can all benefit from the positive impacts of a more diverse, innovative, and accepting society, where everyone has equal opportunities to pursue their dreams and reach their full potential.

#5

Aging and Family Change: Supporting Elderly Family Members Through Transitions

On the Outside

In the past, families in our traditional societies lived in close proximity, and it was expected that they would provide care for their elderly members as a natural part of their responsibilities. However, as modernization and urbanization spread, families became more fragmented and dispersed, making it increasingly challenging to provide adequate care for elderly family members. This shift led to families often being geographically and emotionally distant from their elderly loved ones, making it difficult to provide the necessary care and support.

As a result, there is an increasing need for resources and support for families in caring for their elderly members during transitions such as retirement, illness, and death. There are several challenges that families face when supporting elderly family members through transitions.

I have encountered personally some of the below:

> **Financial constraints**: Financial limitations are a significant challenge when providing care for elderly family members, particularly if they require specialized medical care or assistance with daily living activities that are not covered by healthcare insurance. Families need to make difficult financial decisions and adjust their budgets to ensure that they can provide the necessary support.

Lack of available resources: In some areas, there are shortage of resources, especially skilled ones for home health care services, assisted living facilities, or hospice care. This makes it difficult for families to access the support they need to care for their elderly loved ones.

Legal and logistical issues: When caring for elderly family members, we faced some legal and logistical challenges such as dealing with health insurance policy, managing medical bills and appointments, and making sure that important legal documents like wills and powers of attorney were in place. Having these documents in order helps make sure that healthcare decisions are made based on the elderly person's wishes.

Cultural and social attitudes: When providing care for our elderly loved ones, we encountered challenges related to cultural and social attitudes towards aging and care for the elderly. These attitudes can vary widely, and they sometimes lead to social isolation or stigma for both the elderly person and their caregivers.

Time constraints: Providing care for elderly family members is time-consuming, as we juggle multiple responsibilities such as work, raising children, and caring for our own households. This puts a strain on our time and energy and makes it challenging to provide the necessary care and support.

Multi-city situation: When our parents lived in smaller cities with limited access to good doctors, seeking a second medical opinion was often difficult and expensive, especially during times of medical complications. However, with the advent of 4G internet, following up with healthcare providers became easier and more convenient.

As adult children, the choices we make have a significant impact on the well-being and quality of life of our loved ones. These choices involve difficult decisions about healthcare, finances, and living arrangements, and they may require sacrifices on our part in terms of time, energy, and resources. However, the choices we make also reflect our values and priorities as a family.

On the Inside

As family members age, they may encounter various health challenges that demand specialized attention and care, including chronic illnesses and mobility issues. These challenges create tension within family relationships, requiring everyone involved to adapt their daily routines and expectations.

In my personal experience, I have witnessed how the demands of work and other commitments make it challenging for adult children to provide adequate care and attention to their aging parents. In my family, my mother underwent brain tumor surgery that resulted in a four-month hospitalization. Despite our best efforts, we were unable to bring her back home, and she eventually passed away due to post-surgery complications.

There are several root causes for aging and family change, including:

Demographic changes: According to the World Bank, the life expectancy at birth in India was 32 years in 1947! The current life expectancy has increased to approximately 70 years. As populations age, the number of elderly individuals who require care and support also increases. This puts a strain on families who may be unprepared for the demands of caregiving.

Changes in family structures: Family structures have changed over the years, with more families being geographically dispersed or not adhering to traditional family structures. This makes it more challenging to provide the care and support that their elderly loved ones need.

Changes in societal attitudes: Societal attitudes towards aging and the care of elderly individuals have changed over time. With increasing western influence, there is less emphasis on intergenerational care, with more focus on individualism and personal fulfillment.

Advances in medical care: Advances in medical care have led to longer life expectancies, but also an increase in chronic illnesses and age-related conditions that require specialized care.

Economic factors: Economic factors, such as rising healthcare costs and a lack of affordable care options for elderly family members, makes it difficult for families to provide the necessary support.

The challenges faced by families as they navigate aging and family change are rooted in a complex web of factors. Rapid modernization and urbanization have led to changes in family structures, with many families becoming fragmented and dispersed. This makes it difficult for families to provide care and support for elderly family members who may require specialized attention and care.

What Decisions do you need to consider?

When it comes to supporting elderly family members through transitions, there are several decisions that families may need to consider. In my own experience, my family had to navigate a range of challenges related to balancing our work, finances, and emotional well-being while caring for my mother during her hospitalization. This experience highlighted the significance of being ready to face the challenges that may arise from aging and changes within the family.

When it comes to supporting elderly family members through transitions, there are several decisions that we need to consider.

These include:

Care options: Families need to explore different care options, such as home health care, assisted living facilities, or hospice care, to determine which will best meet their elderly loved ones' needs.

Financial planning: Intentional financial planning is crucial when it comes to providing care for elderly family members, as it can be quite expensive. Families may need to consider their finances and develop a comprehensive plan for covering the costs of care, which may involve factors such as insurance plans, savings, and budget adjustments.

Communication: Effective communication is crucial when caring for elderly family members, and families may need to have frank discussions about everyone's roles, responsibilities, and expectations between siblings and other family members.

Emotional support: Caring for elderly family members is an emotionally taxing affair, and as families we need to prioritize self-care and seek out emotional support from friends, family members, or support groups.

Flexibility: As circumstances change, as families we need to remain flexible and adapt their care plans to meet our loved ones' evolving needs for both physical and emotional wellbeing.

Legal matters: As families we need to ensure that our elderly loved ones have their legal affairs in order, including wills, powers of attorney, and advance directives. Overall, families must make a concerted effort to work together and support each other through the challenges of aging and family change to ensure the best possible outcomes for everyone involved.

What Results you can hope to see:

As we journey through life, one of the most challenging transitions we face is that of aging and family change. Whether it's providing care for elderly parents, dealing with our own aging and health challenges, or navigating the complexities of intergenerational relationships, the transitions that come with aging and family change is indeed difficult to navigate.

In the face of these challenges, it's important to recognize that we are not alone. Families around the world are grappling with these same issues, and there are resources and support available to help us navigate these transitions with compassion, empathy, and resilience.

Supporting elderly family members through transitions lead to a number of positive outcomes.

These may include:

Improved quality of life for the elderly loved one: By providing adequate care and support, our elderly family members enjoy a better quality of life and maintain their independence for longer.

Stronger family relationships: Caring for elderly family members brings family members closer together and strengthens relationships.

Greater emotional well-being: Providing care and support for elderly family members is emotionally taxing, but it can also bring a sense of fulfillment and purpose.

More informed decision-making: By engaging in open and honest communication and seeking out available resources and support, families can make more informed decisions when it comes to the care and support of their elderly loved ones.

Setting an example for younger generations: Present generation children often learn by seeing, and when they see their parents or grandparents providing care and support for elderly family members, it instills values of compassion, empathy, and intergenerational care.

Increased community awareness and support: Caring for elderly family members help raise awareness of the challenges faced by aging individuals and their families, leading to greater community support and resources.

Aging and family transitions require a proactive and compassionate approach. Families must be willing to adapt and seek out resources and support in order to ensure the best possible outcomes for their elderly loved ones. From financial planning to legal considerations, communication, and community support, many factors must be considered when caring for elderly family members.

In the end, it is our commitment to empathy, compassion, and resilience that will guide us through the challenges of aging and family change. By working together as a family and seeking out available resources and support, we ensure the best possible outcomes for our elderly loved ones and maintain strong, healthy family relationships for generations to come.

Ready starters for this Chapter to start implementing:

(Scan this QR for Mental Models, Links to Proven Frameworks and Excel templates to get started)

8

LIFESTYLE AND CHANGE

As a kid, I remember having to create a class routine to capture which day and what class was scheduled. It helped me set the tone for my homework study schedule and even what to pack for tiffin. However, as I matured, I failed to grasp the importance of maintaining a routine. I began avoiding classes that I found dull, which resulted in me skipping school to indulge in play.

But much of whatever little I could achieve later in life is credited to the humble routine that helped me accomplish difficult things. When I consciously brought routine back into my life, it was intentional and deliberate. In "The Compound Effect," Darren Hardy talks about how seemingly inconsequential actions can have a disproportionately large impact over time. This principle can be applied to our lives and habits, as even small changes in our actions in the present could have drastic effects in the future.

Change is a constant and inevitable part of life, and how we adapt to it shapes our future. Some embraced positive lifestyle changes, while others resisted it. Through my experiences and observations, I've gained a deeper appreciation for how lifestyle changes have a profound impact on our personal & professional life.

The intersection of lifestyle and change is a fascinating area of exploration. It's a space where we can see how changes in technology, economy, culture, and society shape our habits, beliefs, and values. In today's world, where change is happening at an unprecedented pace, understanding this becomes even more critical.

In this chapter together, we'll delve into the ways in which lifestyle changes affect our physical and mental health, relationships, careers, and personal growth. We'll explore the challenges and opportunities that come with adapting to new lifestyles and learn to successfully navigate these changes. I hope this chapter serves as a guide for those who seek to make positive changes in their lives and navigate the ever-changing world we live in.

Some key topics on how changes impact your lifestyle

#1. Designing Your Life: How to Use Intentional Planning to Create the Life You Want

#2. Breaking the Cycle of Procrastination: Strategies for Overcoming Inertia

#3. The Power of Self-Reflection: Unlocking Your Potential for Growth and Change

#4. Finding Your Passion: How to Identify and Pursue What Lights You Up

#5. Stuck in a Rut? Overcome Your Limiting Habits and Transform Your Life with Brain Rewiring

#1
Designing Your Life: How to Use Intentional Planning to Create the Life You Want

On the Outside

Have you ever felt like you're just going through the motions of life? Like you're stuck in a rut and don't know how to break free? I have. During my college years, I lived my life without intention, without a clear sense of purpose or direction. I bunked, wandered aimlessly, binged, watched TV, and crashed into bed. For a few years, I didn't have any real goals or dreams, and I didn't feel like I was making any meaningful progress in my life.

It wasn't until I started comparing myself to others that I realized how unhappy I was. I saw friends who were getting into IIMs, some traveling the world, starting their own businesses, and living their best lives. And I experienced a hint of envy and dissatisfaction with my own life. I started to compare my earnings, my relationships, and my accomplishments to theirs, and I felt like I was falling short.

The lack of intentional life planning results in a number of negative external outcomes and experiences, such as:

Lack of direction and purpose: Without clear goals or a sense of direction, we feel aimless and unsure of our path in life. This is not a good space to be in, I have seen many friends getting addicted to substances or ruining their careers, marriage and life.

Procrastination and lack of productivity: Without a clear plan or schedule, I found it difficult to stay focused and productive. This led to procrastination and a sense of not accomplishing anything, which perpetuated a cycle of unproductivity. Eventually, the only way I could feel productive was by engaging in artificial busyness, rather than making meaningful progress towards my goals.

Comparison and envy: Without a clear understanding of our own values and priorities, we are more likely to compare ourselves to others and feel envious of their accomplishments and successes. I felt inadequacy, insecurity, and self-doubt.

Financial instability: Living without a clear plan for managing our finances results in financial instability, leaving us struggling with debt and financial insecurity. I can personally relate to this, as during my college days when I had no clear direction or plan in life, I resorted to lying to my parents for more and more pocket money to support my expenses.

Unfulfilling career or relationships: Without intentional planning and reflection, we end up in careers or relationships that do not align with our values or bring us fulfillment. I have seen breakups occurring on both a personal and professional level due to the lack of intentional planning and reflection.

Lack of intentional life planning leads to a sense of stagnation, unhappiness, and a feeling of being stuck in a rut.

On the Inside

The problem with living without intention is that we can easily fall into this trap of following the herd. We become what we surround ourselves with - the food we eat, the people we spend time with, and the habits we adopt. Every action we take can either be a conscious one or an unconscious one, and if we're not careful, we can end up living a life that doesn't reflect who we truly are. I was astonished to learn that approximately 90% of our daily choices are made without conscious awareness. In Dr. Kahneman's book "Thinking, Fast and Slow," he introduces the idea of two systems: System 1, which functions automatically, and System 2, which demands conscious deliberation. In most cases, we tend to follow the automatic route.

As human beings, we are social creatures. We look to others for cues on how to behave, what to think, and what to aspire to. It's a natural part of our psychology, and it's what has helped us survive and thrive as a species. But sometimes, this follower mentality can lead us astray. It can cause us to make decisions that don't align with our true desires or values, simply because we're following the crowd.

Living without intention leads us to follow the herd and adopt habits, behaviors, and paths that do not align with our true selves.

This occurs due to several root causes, such as:

Lack of self-awareness: If we do not know ourselves well enough, we struggle to identify our goals, values, and priorities, which makes it challenging to create a clear plan for our life. It's important to know ourselves and our current identities before attempting to change them. This requires inward focus and self-awareness.

Fear of failure: When we are afraid of failing or making mistakes, we avoid taking risks or pursuing our dreams, which prevent us from designing a fulfilling life. I found instead of focusing on the fear of failure, it is more productive to work on maximizing the chances of success by taking calculated risks and learning from any mistakes along the way.

Lack of Purpose: Motivation is a feeling that comes and goes, and it's not always reliable for long-term success. To achieve long-term success, it's important to develop habits and systems that support our goals, even when our motivation wanes.

External pressures: We may feel pressure from societal expectations, family, or friends, which lead us to pursue paths that do not align with our true desires or passions. FOMO (Fear of Missing Out) lead us to compare ourselves to others and feel like we're missing out on experiences or opportunities, which can cause us to make choices that don't align with our true values or priorities.

Short-term thinking: If we only focus on immediate gratification rather than long-term goals, we may struggle to create a cohesive plan for our life that leads to sustained fulfillment and success.

Identifying these root causes and working to address them help us overcome the barriers to intentional life planning and design. By doing so, we create a life that aligns with our true desires, values, and passions, and lead a fulfilling and purposeful existence.

What Decisions do you need to consider?

Have you ever felt like you're just going through the motions of life, without a clear sense of purpose or direction? It's a common experience, and it can be easy to fall into the trap of living a life that doesn't reflect who we truly are. But being not intentional is also a decision - just a really bad one. It's a decision to let circumstances dictate our lives, rather than taking control and creating the life we want.

To live with intention is to be honest with ourselves, to take accountability for our actions and the results we hope to achieve. It's about setting meaningful goals and taking purposeful steps towards them.

Below are some strategies that helped me create a life that reflects my values and passions, instead of blindly following others.

Identify your values and priorities: Understanding what truly matters to you is essential in creating a fulfilling life. Take time to reflect on your values and priorities, and make sure they align with your goals and aspirations. Create a list of non-negotiables in life, the things you refuse to compromise on, no matter what.

Define your life goals: Once you know your values and priorities, define your long-term and short-term goals. The SMART framework helps you focus on creating goals that are clear, concise, and easy to track progress towards. It stands for Specific, Measurable, Achievable, Relevant, and Time-bound and helps define the WHAT part of goal setting.

Create an execution plan: Develop a plan that outlines the steps you need to take to achieve your goals. Break them down into smaller, manageable tasks and set deadlines for each one. Use PACT framework to create a purposeful, actionable, continuous and trackable plan and help define the HOW part of the goal setting.

Establish a routine: Creating a routine supports our goals and aligns with your values and priorities. This helps to stay focused and consistent in our efforts. There will be days you can't stick to the routine, it's ok.

Forgive yourself and move to the next day. It's a numbers game, the more you repeat and build consistency the more you get better at it and grow.

Stay accountable: Hold yourself accountable for your progress by tracking your achievements, celebrating your successes, and learning from your mistakes. Capturing defining moments with selfies and keeping a Happy memory box, where I wrote down my achievements and happy moments on paper chits, helped boost my morale and served as a reminder of my progress during tough times.

Adapt to change: Life is unpredictable, and it's essential to be flexible and adaptable. Be willing to adjust your goals and plans as needed and embrace new opportunities that align with your values and priorities.

Seek support: Building a fulfilling life requires support from others. Surround yourself with people who encourage and inspire you, and seek guidance from mentors or coaches if needed. Remember that transformation is hard, so having an accountability partner to share your journey with and enjoy a laugh together can make all the difference.

As a seeker of happiness, you may be tempted to take shortcuts and find quick fixes for your problems. But true happiness is not something that can be achieved through external means alone. It's an inside job, and it requires us to cultivate a sense of inner peace and contentment that is not dependent on external circumstances.

I find it intriguing to explore and gain insights from the wisdom imparted in the ancient literature and philosophy of India, Japan and China. These ageless works serve as a reminder that the key to genuine happiness and contentment is to live our lives with intention and purpose. By giving importance to self-awareness, focusing on our strengths, and aligning our actions with our values, we can intentionally create a life that is meaningful and gratifying. It may require consistent and conscious effort, but by taking these steps, we can shape our life journey in a more positive and purposeful direction.

What Results you can hope to see:

Have you ever set a goal for yourself, only to find yourself struggling to achieve it? It's a common experience, and it can be frustrating to feel like you're not making progress towards what you want. But what if there was a simple yet powerful tool you could use to help you achieve your goals?

That tool is working backwards. Seeing the results, you want to achieve and then working backwards to figure out the steps you need to take to get there. It's a simple concept, but it's one that successful people have used to their advantage in both their personal and professional lives.

When we work backwards, we're able to break down our goals into manageable steps. We can identify the obstacles that are standing in our way and come up with strategies to overcome them. We can also create a clear roadmap for ourselves, which can help us stay motivated and focused on our goals.

Designing your life with intentional planning lead to a variety of positive outcomes, such as:

Increased fulfillment and happiness: Living a life that aligns with your own values and passions increases your sense of fulfillment and happiness, as you are working towards goals that truly matter to you.

Greater sense of purpose: Knowing what matters most to us and having a clear plan for achieving those goals gives a sense of purpose and direction in life.

Improved productivity and success: By setting clear goals and creating a plan to achieve them, we become more productive and achieve greater success in our personal and professional life.

Better financial stability: With intentional planning, we can create a budget and financial plan that aligns with our values and goals, which leads to greater financial stability and security.

Stronger relationships: By surrounding ourselves with people who support and inspire us, and by being intentional about our relationships, we can build stronger and more meaningful connections with others.

Working backwards can be a challenging process. It requires us to be honest with ourselves about what we truly want, and it asks us to commit to a process that may not always be easy. But, the rewards of intentional living are significant. By creating a clear vision for our lives, setting meaningful goals, and taking purposeful steps towards achieving them, we can create a life that is aligned with our values and passions.

But this journey towards intentional living is not a one-time event. It's a lifelong process of self-discovery, growth, and change. It requires us to be willing to adapt and adjust our plans as we go, to learn from our failures and setbacks, and to stay focused on what truly matters to us.

Although we may not have achieved the traditional markers of success that society recognizes, living a life aligned with our values and passions still brings you a deep sense of contentment and fulfillment, which is a truly wonderful state to be in.

#2

Breaking the Cycle of Procrastination: Strategies for Overcoming Inertia

On the Outside

Thanks to evolution and our city lives, there are no wild predators, nor more dependence on weather for food, we have clothes to beat the sun and cold. As humans we have hacked the planet earth! Now with modern city life, we are more comfortable than ever before. We can get most things done with a few taps and clicks.

The convenience and ease of modern city life leads to a lack of motivation or urgency to complete tasks. When everything is easily accessible and readily available, it is tempting to put off important responsibilities and engage in more enjoyable or entertaining activities instead. I found this as one of the key factors where procrastination comes into play.

Procrastination is the act of delaying or postponing tasks that need to be completed, often to the point of causing negative consequences. It is not the same as taking breaks, prioritizing tasks, or delegating responsibilities. It manifests in various forms, such as watching TV instead of studying or working, browsing social media instead of completing a project, or delaying important decisions. `

Procrastination presents itself in many different forms, and the symptoms and experiences vary from person to person.

Here are some common examples of how procrastination shows up externally.

Delayed or missed deadlines: I struggled to meet deadlines for work, during college, or personal projects. This results in missed opportunities, lost income, and damaged relationships.

Poor performance: Procrastination leads to rushed or incomplete work, which results in lower quality output or poorer grades.

Increased stress and anxiety: The pressure of looming deadlines and unfinished work leads to stress and anxiety, which further contribute to procrastination and the cycle continues.

Overwhelming to-do lists: Procrastination causes tasks to pile up, leading to an overwhelming to-do list that feels impossible to complete.

Time-wasting behaviors: When procrastination sets in, it's common to engage in time-wasting behaviors that can be counterproductive, such as scrolling through social media or binge-watching TV shows instead of completing necessary tasks.

Difficulty with prioritization: Procrastination results in a lack of focus and direction, and struggle in determining which tasks are most important or urgent. We may find ourselves feeling overwhelmed or unable to make progress on our goals.

Negative self-talk: Procrastination leads to feelings of guilt, shame, and self-doubt, which further contribute to a cycle of procrastination.

Procrastination stems from a variety of reasons, such as a lack of interest or motivation, feeling overwhelmed, lacking necessary skills or resources, poor time-management or organization, and perfectionism or indecisiveness. Identifying the root cause of procrastination is key to developing effective strategies for overcoming it.

On the Inside

Learning about how our brain works is a fascinating subject. Our brain has evolved to keep us safe, protected, and comfortable at all times. Its ultimate responsibility is to ensure our survival, and it works tirelessly to achieve this goal. When confronted with a potentially uncomfortable or risky situation, our brain goes into action mode and uses its survival instincts to keep us safe. However, the brain can't always distinguish between real physical threats, such as facing a herd of tigers, and non-threatening situations, such as giving a speech in front of a large audience. As a result, it may try to discourage us from taking risks, even when they are necessary for personal growth and success.

There are several underlying causes of procrastination, and it can vary from person to person.

Here are some common factors that contribute:

Fear of failure: The fear of failing or not meeting one's own or others' expectations leads to procrastination as a way of avoiding the possibility of failure. In my college, I avoided studying Math paper only to fail and re-appear next semester's arrear paper.

Perfectionism: I tried to build the perfect solution for my customers, but in doing so, I missed the opportunity to go to market and lost out to competitors. Striving for perfection leads to procrastination, as we may avoid starting or completing a task if we feel like it's not perfect yet.

Lack of motivation or interest: Have you ever found yourself feeling overwhelmed and stressed as a deadline approached, with little motivation to complete a project? When a task is not enjoyable or interesting to us, we tend to put it off in favor of more enjoyable or interesting activities.

Overwhelm: I have personally experienced how overwhelm can lead to procrastination. During my first job, my manager used to assign tasks to me without providing adequate guidance or support. As a result, I often felt overwhelmed by the complexity of the tasks and struggled to know where to start. This caused me to avoid starting or completing the tasks, as they felt too daunting and unmanageable.

Lack of clarity or direction: It's important to have a clear understanding of what needs to be done and how to do it in order to avoid procrastination and achieve success in completing the task. Seeking clarity is important whether from a teacher, mentor or boss.

Poor time-management skills: We may procrastinate due to poor time-management skills, such as underestimating how much time is needed to complete a task or getting easily distracted. It takes 23 mins approx. to get back focus once we are distracted.

Low self-esteem or confidence: It's not uncommon for us to procrastinate due to low self-esteem or confidence, feeling like we are not capable of completing the task or that our efforts will not be good enough.

Procrastination is caused by a combination of many factors, and identifying the root cause requires some self-reflection and introspection. By understanding the underlying reasons for procrastination, we can take steps to address these factors and develop strategies for overcoming them.

What Decisions do you need to consider?

As someone who has struggled with procrastination in the past, I know firsthand how challenging it can be to break the cycle of putting things off. In my previous job, I found myself constantly procrastinating on important tasks, leading to increased stress and missed deadlines. It wasn't until I made a series of deliberate decisions and took specific actions that I was able to successfully beat procrastination and achieve my goals.

One of the key decisions I made was to approach my tasks in a more manageable way. I broke down larger projects into smaller, more achievable steps, which reduced overwhelm and increased my motivation to act. I also worked on reframing my mindset and beliefs about my ability to complete the task, focusing on the positive and empowering aspects of my work.

I also made changes to my environment and habits to reduce distractions and increase productivity. I created a dedicated workspace and eliminated potential triggers that could lead to procrastination. I set specific goals and schedules, took regular breaks, and engaged in self-care activities to reduce stress and maintain my energy levels.

Here's my personal checklist for overcoming procrastination:

Create your new identity: To create a new identity and overcome procrastination, use the identity-based habits model. This involves identifying the person you want to become, developing new habits that align with your desired identity, and taking small actions consistently to reinforce your new identity.

Set specific goals: Set clear, measurable goals for each task, with deadlines and criteria for success. I used S.M.A.R.T goals for setting WHAT needs to be done and P.A.C.T to define HOW to get there.

Prioritize tasks: Decide which tasks are most important and tackle those first. I used the Eisenhower Matrix to categorize tasks based on their importance and urgency.

Eliminate distractions: Remove potential distractions from your environment, such as turning off notifications on your phone. Use the 5S model to remove potential distractions from your environment.

Take regular breaks: Rest and recharge by taking regular breaks throughout the day. I am a big fan of Pomodoro Technique to break down each task into smaller, more manageable steps. This helps to work in shorter, more focused bursts and take breaks in between creating daily progress.

Engage in self-care activities: Mindfulness meditation, such as the body scan practice, is an effective self-care activity for reducing stress and overcoming procrastination. By focusing on each part of the body and noticing sensations, you can increase awareness and promote relaxation.

By intentionally training my brain and making deliberate decisions about how I approached my tasks, mindset, environment, and habits, I was able to successfully beat procrastination and achieve greater success in my work.

What Results you can hope to see:

Procrastination is a silent killer of dreams, goals and ambitions. It stops us from achieving the success we desire and deserve. We often put off important tasks until the last minute, or worse, never complete them at all. By breaking the cycle of procrastination, we can achieve our goals with confidence and live a life without the baggage of regrets.

Here are some results you can hope to see by breaking the cycle of procrastination:

Increased productivity: By overcoming procrastination and taking action on important tasks, we increase our productivity and accomplish more in less time.

Improved time management: By setting clear goals and priorities, creating a plan, and eliminating distractions, we better manage our time and make the most of our day.

Reduced stress: By breaking down large tasks into smaller steps and taking regular breaks, I reduced my stress and prevented burnout despite taking on tough challenges.

Greater sense of accomplishment: By setting specific goals and achieving them, we can experience a greater sense of accomplishment and satisfaction.

Improved self-confidence: By overcoming procrastination and taking action on important tasks, we can improve our self-confidence and belief in our abilities.

More free time: By being more productive and efficient, I found more free time to pursue other interests and hobbies, such as writing this book!

Remember, breaking the cycle of procrastination is a journey, not a destination. It requires consistent effort and a willingness to face challenges and setbacks along the way. But by taking small steps each day and staying focused on your goals, you can achieve lasting change and experience greater success and fulfillment in your personal and professional life. So, keep moving forward, and never give up on the power of progress and growth.

#3
The Power of Self-Reflection: Unlocking Your Potential for Growth and Change

On the Outside

For a long time, my identity has been rooted in the habit of looking outward to find issues and assign blame to others for not making enough progress in my life. I found fault with the government, my employer, family members, and even the mosquito that bit me. Regrettably, I never directed my attention inward to examine my own thoughts, beliefs, and actions.

I lacked insight into my own thoughts, feelings, and actions, and I was either unwilling or unable to learn and grow from my personal experiences. As a result, I tended to compare myself with others and sought fulfillment through material possessions as a source of satisfaction and validation in an always busy environment that I had cluttered and created myself.

Lack of self-reflection can be attributed to several factors, some include:

Busy lifestyle: When we have a busy and hectic lifestyle, it can be challenging to find time to pause and reflect on our thoughts and actions. This may be especially true for those who work long hours or have a lot of responsibilities at home.

Negative environment: If we are in an environment that is unsupportive, critical, or negative, we may feel defensive and less likely to reflect on our behavior. When we feel judged or attacked by those around us, we may be less likely to engage in self-reflection.

Lack of feedback: Without feedback from others, it can be difficult for us to assess our own behavior and understand how we are perceived by others. If we don't receive feedback, we may assume that our actions and behaviors are acceptable and may not engage in self-reflection.

Distractions: In today's digital age, distractions such as social media, television, and other forms of entertainment can make it challenging to focus on introspection and self-reflection. Constant stimulation prevents us from being fully present with ourselves and our thoughts.

Success and achievement: Ironically, success and achievement can also be external factors that contribute to a lack of self-reflection. If we are constantly praised for our accomplishments, we may not feel the need to reflect on our behavior and make changes. This can lead to complacency and a lack of personal growth.

On the Inside

In the game of life, we are all players seeking to maximize our happiness and well-being. However, the pursuit of happiness can sometimes lead us down a path of comparison, jealousy, ego, and frustration. When we focus too much on external factors such as wealth, status, and material possessions, we get caught in a vicious cycle of competition and comparison, where we see the world as a zero-sum game in which our success depends on the failure of others.

This conditioning can start early on, in the modern school system, where students are often pitted against each other in a competitive environment that prioritizes grades, sports, and other achievements. In game theory, this is known as a zero-sum game, where one player's gain is another player's loss. This mindset can carry over into adulthood, where we continue to view success and happiness as a limited resource that must be fought for and won at the expense of others.

I have experienced the below as the profound underlying causes of lack of self-reflection:

An external focus may lead to a lack of introspection and self-reflection, causing us to prioritize material possessions, status, and achievement over personal growth.

Fear of vulnerability makes it difficult for us to examine our own thoughts, emotions, and behaviors, as it requires a willingness to acknowledge and confront personal weaknesses and shortcomings.

Negative conditioning, such as criticism, rejection, and failure, lead us to adopt a defensive mindset that hinders self-reflection and personal growth.

Without mindfulness, we struggle to observe our own thoughts, emotions, and behaviors objectively, making self-reflection more challenging.

Strong ego and defensiveness make it difficult for us to accept criticism and acknowledge personal shortcomings, hindering self-reflection and personal growth.

Our busy lifestyles make it challenging to find time for self-reflection and introspection, as it requires a dedicated and intentional effort to set aside time for reflection.

This mentality leads to a lack of self-reflection, as we become so focused on external factors and winning the game that we forget to examine our own thoughts, emotions, and behaviors. In order to break out of this cycle and achieve true fulfillment and happiness, we must learn to shift our focus inward and cultivate self-awareness and personal growth.

By recognizing that true happiness comes from within, we can break free from the zero-sum game mentality and develop a more positive and fulfilling outlook on life. Through self-reflection and introspection, we can gain a deeper understanding of ourselves and our place in the world, and work towards creating a more harmonious and fulfilling existence for ourselves and others.

What Decisions do you need to consider?

In Robert Louis Stevenson's novel "Strange Case of Dr. Jekyll and Mr. Hyde," he tells the story of a man who creates a potion that turns him into a sinister alter ego named Mr. Hyde. The novel explores themes of duality, identity, and the human psyche.

Just as Dr. Jekyll and Mr. Hyde are two sides of the same person, our inner selves have two distinct voices - one that represents our higher aspirations and another that embodies our darker impulses. When we turn our focus inward and confront our inner Mr. Hyde, we gain control over our emotions and become more aware of the underlying reasons behind our actions. We gain insight into the beliefs that shape our choices and decisions, which in turn allows us to be more present and mindful in the moment. By taking responsibility for our present actions and choices, we shape our future self-piece by piece, and become who we aspire to be.

Overcoming a lack of self-reflection involves making a series of decisions and commitments to prioritize introspection and personal growth.

Here are some decisions that one might consider:

Commit to self-reflection: The first step is to make a conscious decision to prioritize introspection and personal growth. This involves setting aside time for reflection, engaging in mindfulness practices, or seeking feedback from others.

Challenge negative self-talk: Taking a decision to challenge negative thoughts and replace them with positive, growth-oriented ones help cultivate a more introspective mindset.

Cultivate self-awareness: Developing greater self-awareness helps us recognize our own thoughts, emotions, and behaviors, and identify areas for personal growth. Deciding to prioritize self-awareness involves engaging in mindfulness practices, seeking feedback from others, and writing a journal. I prefer writing with pen and paper.

Practice vulnerability: Embracing vulnerability helps us confront personal weaknesses and shortcomings, and promote greater self-reflection and personal growth. Deciding to practice vulnerability involves seeking feedback from others, acknowledging mistakes, and being open to constructive criticism.

Let go of the need for control: The need for control can hinder self-reflection and personal growth by creating a defensive mindset. Deciding to let go of the need for control and embrace uncertainty and vulnerability promotes greater self-awareness and ultimately personal growth.

Foster a growth mindset: By adopting a growth mindset, I am able to focus on learning and personal growth rather than fixed traits and abilities. This mindset encourages me to seek out challenges, embrace failure as a learning opportunity, and prioritize personal development over external validation.

Writing is the secret superpower for high achievers. By reflecting on our experiences through journaling, we gain clarity and perspective on our thoughts and emotions, identify negative patterns of thought, and challenge and reframe negative beliefs. Regular journaling also helps to reduce stress and anxiety, enhance creativity, and promote greater self-awareness and personal development.

I find my journal a safe and confidential place where I can bounce back from setbacks and reflect on my experiences, thoughts, and emotions. It serves as a powerful tool for self-reflection and personal growth, helping me to overcome obstacles and get better at it every day. So, embrace the power of writing and start your own journal today.

Like most great things, writing in a journal may sound simple and unexciting. However, I want to emphasize that this is an open secret to personal growth and development. The key is to make a start and maintain a routine, forgiving yourself if you fall behind on some days, and getting back at it the next day. By staying committed to this practice, you can gain profound self-awareness and approach life with a new perspective.

What Results you can hope to see:

No matter how many books I read or watched YouTube videos, I have found it challenging to stay motivated and consistent. To help overcome when I started tracking my actions, I was able to report back to myself and identify areas where I needed to adjust. Without this report back system, I've found it difficult to see the real benefits of my efforts and have struggled to stay committed to my self-improvement goals.

Implementing this tracking system has been a game-changer for me. It helps me to stay accountable and motivated, and to recognize the progress I'm making, even on days when it feels like I'm not making much headway. With this system in place, I'm able to stay focused on my goals and approach my journey of self-reflection and personal growth with renewed enthusiasm and purpose.

By journaling your day and implementing a tracking system for self-reflection and personal growth, there are several positive results that you can see happening for you:

- **Greater self-awareness**: Tracking our actions help us to identify patterns and trends in our behavior, allowing us to gain greater insight into your thoughts, emotions, and actions.
- **Increased motivation**: Intrinsic motivation is more powerful and effective than external motivation. Seeing progress towards our goals helps to keep us motivated and committed to our self-improvement journey.
- **Improved accountability**: Having a tracking system in place helps in holding us accountable for our own actions and ensures that we're taking the necessary steps towards creating a better version of ourselves.
- **Enhanced goal-setting**: Regular tracking helps in refining and adjusting our goals as needed, ensuring that we're working towards the objectives that are meaningful and achievable.
- **Positive mindset**: By tracking our progress and recognizing our accomplishments, we experience a greater sense of positivity and well-being, leading to enhanced resilience and overall mental health.

Self-reflection is a powerful tool for personal growth and development. By taking the time to reflect on our thoughts, emotions, and actions, we gain greater self-awareness, identify areas for improvement, and cultivate a more positive and growth-oriented mindset.

Through journaling, tracking our progress, and embracing a growth mindset, we can overcome obstacles, build resilience, and reach our full potential. By focusing on intrinsic motivation and personal interests, we tap into a powerful source of motivation and drive that sustains us over the long term.

While the journey of self-reflection and personal growth may not always be easy, the rewards are immeasurable. By investing in ourselves and committing to our own personal growth, we create a more fulfilling, meaningful, and joyful life for ourselves and those around us.

#4
Finding Your Passion: How to Identify and Pursue What Lights You Up

On the Outside

The German word for passion, "Leidenschaft," literally translates to "the ability to hardship." It refers to an activity that you can do day in and out, repeatedly, and still find happiness in doing it. This activity may or may not provide any monetary reward, but you still want to dedicate your time and focus to it. I found introverted individuals too becoming more animated and sociable when discussing their passions.

If you haven't found your passion yet, chances are you're feeling lost, unfulfilled, or dissatisfied with your life. It could be due to a lack of clarity and intentionality in your pursuits or a sense of aimlessness or confusion about your goals and aspirations.

We may experience a lack of passion, which can manifest in a variety of ways:

Lack of enthusiasm: We may find it difficult to get excited or motivated about anything, and everything may seem like a chore. Others perceive us as disinterested or apathetic.

Procrastination: This has been a struggle for me for many years. I've found myself making countless excuses to delay or avoid studying, putting off important tasks or projects, and struggling to meet deadlines or achieve my goals.

Boredom: We may feel like our life lacks meaning or purpose, and struggle to find enjoyment in our daily activities. Unfortunately, resorting to distractions like Netflix or video games can make things worse and perpetuate a vicious cycle.

Low energy: We may feel tired, lethargic, or unmotivated, and struggle to find the energy to pursue new interests or activities. Energy attracts energy and the lack of energy attracts similar low-energy individuals into our lives, a cycle hard to break.

Lack of direction: We may feel unsure about what we want to do with your life, and struggle to set clear goals or priorities. In a fast-paced world, this can lead us to move quickly in the wrong direction, ultimately causing us to feel lost and unfulfilled.

Negative mindset: We may feel stuck or trapped in our current situation, and struggle to see the possibilities for change or growth. Over time, a negative mindset can become a self-fulfilling prophecy, leading us to make choices that reinforce our negative beliefs.

Unfulfillment: Feeling like something is missing in our life? Lack of passion leads to struggles to find meaning or satisfaction in our work or relationships.

Focusing solely on the problems and challenges leads to a sense of hopelessness and defeat. It is important to remember that challenges and setbacks are a natural part of life. Rather than getting discouraged by them, we can use them as opportunities for learning and growth. By reframing challenges as opportunities, we can turn them into catalysts for positive change and transformation.

On the Inside

As a child, I was always curious and loved to play with toys. I had collections of GI Joe, He-Man, and other action figures, which I would break apart and use to build my own creations. Thanks to the supportive environment I grew up in, I had the opportunity to try out many different things, and even got paid for some of them before eventually settling into my profession.

Being passionate about something can be both a blessing and a curse. On the one hand, it gives us the drive and confidence to pursue our dreams, even when the odds of success are low. Without that overconfidence, I doubt I would have ever taken the leap into entrepreneurship, which is notorious for its high failure rates. On the other hand, passion can also blind you to the realities of the situation, making it easy to be exploited at work or to take on undesirable tasks or work overtime.

We lack passion in life because we have not found activities or interests that truly inspire us. Some of the root causes include:

Fear: Fear of failure, fear of success, fear of change, fear of the unknown, and fear of rejection all prevent us from pursuing our passions.

Lack of self-awareness: Without knowing our strengths, weaknesses, interests, and values, it is challenging to identify what we're passionate about.

Negative mindset: A negative mindset leads to feelings of doubt, self-criticism, and hopelessness, making it difficult to find motivation and passion.

Lack of exposure: If we haven't been exposed to different experiences, hobbies, or careers, we may not know what we're passionate about.

Social and cultural conditioning: Society and culture influence our beliefs, values, and expectations, which may not align with our true passions and desires.

Whether it's fear, boredom, low energy, a lack of direction, or a negative mindset, these challenges can all hold us back from achieving our full potential.

But it's also important to remember that these obstacles can be overcome. By cultivating a growth mindset, setting clear goals, and taking small steps towards positive change, we can begin to build momentum and create a more fulfilling and meaningful life for ourselves.

What Decisions do you need to consider?

To overcome the lack of passion, it is important to make decisions that are centered on focusing on what you care about rather than just what you love. This means aligning your passion with your values and the impact you want to have, even if the tasks associated with it are not enjoyable or mundane. Focusing solely on happiness may not sustain your interest in an endeavor in the long run, but focusing on how it helps you achieve what you care about will. Resilience is also key in pursuing your passion, as it can be a challenging and ongoing process.

By making intentional decisions and staying committed to the impact you want to make, you can overcome the lack of passion and find fulfillment in your pursuits.

Focusing on what you care about: Instead of just focusing on what you love or enjoy, consider aligning your passion with your values and the impact you want to have. Instead, use your values and desired impact as the true north on your compass, and let that guide your passion. It's like taking a journey to a destination you care about, even if the journey itself may not always be enjoyable.

Recognizing that passion wanes over time: While it's important to pursue something you are passionate about, keep in mind that passion can fade over time. Therefore, it's crucial to also focus on how your pursuit helps you achieve what you care about in the long term.

Building resilience: Pursuing your passion can be a challenging and ongoing process that requires resilience. Be prepared to face setbacks and obstacles along the way, and develop the resilience to overcome them and stay committed to your pursuit.

Balancing passion with practicality: While it's important to follow your passion, it's also important to consider practical considerations such as financial stability, personal responsibilities, and other commitments. Finding a balance between pursuing your passion and meeting these practical needs help ensure short-term and long-term success and fulfillment.

Being open to learning and growth: Pursuing your passion often involves stepping out of your comfort zone and taking risks. Be open to learning new skills, seeking out feedback and guidance, and embracing growth opportunities to help you achieve your goals.

What Results you can hope to see:

We all have passions and things that excite us. For some, it may be a hobby or a sport, while for others, it could be a particular cause or profession. When we pursue our passions, we feel more alive, energized, and fulfilled. It's like finding the missing piece of a puzzle that completes the picture.

But it's not just about feeling good at the moment. Pursuing our passions has significant long-term benefits in our lives. It leads to increased creativity, productivity, and a sense of purpose. It also improves our mental and physical health, as we engage in activities that bring us joy and reduce stress.

By identifying and pursuing your passion, you can experience a variety of positive outcomes in your personal and professional life.

Here are some potential results to look forward to:

Increased happiness and fulfillment: Pursuing something you are passionate about brings joy and meaning to our lives, leading to increased happiness and fulfillment.

Improved mental and physical health: Engaging in activities you are passionate about have positive effects on both your mental and physical health, reducing stress and improving overall well-being.

Increased motivation and productivity: When we are passionate about something, we are more likely to be motivated to work towards our goals and be productive in our pursuits.

Increased creativity and innovation: Pursuing our passion sparks creativity and innovation, leading to new ideas and solutions in all spheres of your life.

Increased confidence and self-esteem: Pursuing our passion and achieving the goals boosts our confidence and self-esteem, giving us a sense of accomplishment and pride in our abilities.

As I reflect on writing this book, I realize how much it has helped me grow and overcome my own struggles. Writing has always been a passion for me, and it has brought me success in various aspects of my professional life. But when I set out to write this book, I faced challenges like negative thoughts, lack of focus, and balancing family responsibilities.

What kept me going was the impact I wanted to make in the lives of one million people who face similar struggles. My personal values of impact, growth, hustle, and excellence aligned with this goal. This helped me establish a daily routine of writing, without worrying about the outcome, because I knew that what I felt inside me needed to come out.

The journey was not easy, but it was worth it. Whether you're a student, job seeker, professional, aspiring entrepreneur, or mid-management employee, it's important to find your passion and pursue it with dedication and resilience. You may face challenges, but when you stay focused on your cause driven passions and values, you can and you will overcome them and achieve success.

#5
Stuck in a Rut? Overcome Your Limiting Habits and Transform Your Life with Brain Rewiring

On the Outside

Have you ever found yourself stuck in a pattern of behavior that's holding you back from achieving your goals? I have struggled personally with procrastination, overeating, and negative self-talk. Whatever your limiting habits may be, it's not easy to break free from them and create new habits that serve you better.

Habits are automatic behaviors that we perform without much conscious thought or effort, and they're often deeply rooted in our past experiences and environment. Our current habits are deeply ingrained in our brains and bodies, making them difficult to change.

When we try to change our habits, we often face a number of challenges and obstacles. We feel overwhelmed by the effort required to break old patterns of behavior and develop new ones. We struggle with consistency and motivation, finding it difficult to stick with our new habits over the long term.

And we may encounter setbacks and obstacles along the way, causing us to doubt our ability to create lasting change.

Some external symptoms that may indicate being stuck with limiting habits are:

Lack of progress towards achieving personal or professional goals

Feeling stuck or trapped in a routine that is not serving your best interests

Health problems or negative consequences resulting from unhealthy habits, such as overeating, smoking, or substance abuse.

Social isolation or relationship problems resulting from habits that interfere with interpersonal connections

Financial problems resulting from poor money management habits

Poor time management skills resulting from procrastination or other limiting habits

Frustration, stress, and feelings of helplessness due to the inability to break free from old habits

Low self-esteem, negative self-talk, or other psychological symptoms resulting from negative habits

Have you ever found yourself in any of these situations? I can relate to all of them, having experienced them at various points in my life. It's a challenging and uncomfortable place to be. As much as we value our independence and freedom, our limiting habits hold us back and leave us feeling trapped in a cycle of repetitive behavior, like a lab rat that has become conditioned to its environment. Despite our physical freedom, we feel mentally trapped, unable to break free from these patterns and move forward.

On the Inside

Tasks that fall below our abilities can feel monotonous, whereas those that exceed our abilities can lead to anxiety or a sense of being overwhelmed. In city life, our brains have been trained to take the easiest and most efficient route possible in order to conserve energy and protect ourselves. However, this mindset can impede us from completing important routines or tasks that contribute to our growth. Our brains tend to calculate the effort required and send signals to delay or avoid them. With awareness of these patterns, we can overcome them and retrain our brains to prioritize intentional action.

Identifying and working through the internal factors is necessary for overcoming limiting habits and building new, positive behaviors.

Here are some of the internal causes of limiting habits:

Lack of self-awareness: For a long time, I was not fully aware of my own habits and how they impact my daily life. Without recognizing my limiting habits, it was challenging to make changes and move towards more positive behaviors.

Fear of change: Change can be scary, and many of us fear the uncertainty and discomfort that come with making significant changes to their habits and routines. This fear prevents us from acting and making the necessary changes to overcome our limiting habits.

Lack of motivation: Even when we recognize the need for change, we struggle with staying motivated and committed to new habits. This lack of motivation can be caused by a variety of factors, including negative self-talk and a lack of accountability.

Poor self-discipline: Building new habits requires consistent effort and discipline. Many of us struggle with staying disciplined and may find it challenging to maintain new habits over time.

Ineffective coping mechanisms: Limiting habits often develop as coping mechanisms to deal with stress or difficult emotions. Without effective alternatives, we may continue to rely on these habits even when they recognize their negative impact.

Habit Loop: Habits are often deeply ingrained in our neural pathways, and it can be difficult to break the habit loop that connects the cue, the behavior, and the reward. People may need to rewire their brains by developing new habits and routines to replace old ones.

The human brain is wired to default to habitual actions as a way of conserving energy. This means that our behavior today has a significant impact on our future actions and the formation of our habits. Through repetition and practice, activities that once felt challenging can become effortless and automatic, such as driving a car, coding, or cooking.

What Decisions do you need to consider?

To make progress towards our goals, we must combine knowledge with consistent action. This creates momentum and leads to the development of automated habits that make progress effortless. However, it's important to acknowledge that our natural tendency towards habitual behavior can also hinder our growth when we have limiting habits that hold us back.

To overcome these limiting habits, we must take intentional action and be willing to step out of our comfort zones. By recognizing the power of repetition in forming and breaking habits, we can make deliberate decisions and develop new, positive behaviors that serve us better in the long run.

So, when considering the decisions that will lead us towards our goals, it's important to keep in mind the role of habits in our lives. By intentionally choosing and cultivating positive habits, we can transform our behavior and create a more fulfilling life for ourselves.

Our identity is a powerful force that shapes our beliefs, attitudes, and behaviors. It's no wonder that we will go to great lengths to preserve it, even if it means holding onto habits that no longer serve us. One key lesson from the book 'Atomic Habits' is that in order to replace bad habits with good ones, it's important to focus on identity change rather than just behavior change. In other words, you need to shift your self-image to that of a person who already has the habits you want to develop.

Here are some steps you can take to make this shift:

Define the identity you want to have: Start by identifying the habits you want to develop and the type of person you want to become. Ask yourself: Who do I want to be? What kind of person has the habits I want to develop? For example, if you want to become a fitter person, you might define yourself as someone who is physically active, has the energy for both professional and family life, and maybe run a 10k marathon!

Visualize yourself in this new identity: Take some time to imagine what it would look and feel like to be the person you want to become. See yourself exercising regularly, eating healthy foods, or whatever habits you want to develop. Imagine the positive outcomes that will result from these habits and how they will improve your life.

Start small: Begin by taking small actions that align with your new identity. For example, if you want to become a regular exerciser, start by doing 10 minutes of exercise each day. As you start to see yourself as a person who exercises regularly, you can gradually increase the duration and intensity of your workouts.

Use positive affirmations: Affirmations are powerful statements that help to reinforce your new identity. Write down affirmations in present tense that align with your new identity and repeat them to yourself every day. Write as if you have already become the person you aspire to be. For example, "I am a person who exercises regularly and enjoys being active."

Celebrate your successes: When you take actions that align with your new identity, celebrate them! This will help to reinforce your new habits and identity. For example, if you exercise regularly for a week, treat yourself to a small reward like a movie or shopping for something nice for yourself.

The key to making sustainable changes is to avoid overwhelming ourselves with sudden, drastic alterations that may lead to failure. Instead, we can focus on making small, consistent progress towards our desired outcomes. By doing so, we can develop new habits that align with our desired identity and ultimately lead to lasting change.

In the world of software development, prototyping is a crucial technique that enables stakeholders to review the design and functionality of a product before its implementation. This method helps to avoid major changes or issues down the line, ultimately saving time and resources. Similarly, in our personal lives, we can use visualization exercises to create a new identity and make any necessary adjustments before fully committing to it and gradually work towards our goals.

What Results you can hope to see:

I used to love eating anything and everything, but my unhealthy food choices eventually led to weight gain and lifestyle diseases. To break free from this cycle, I had to resist the temptation of indulging in my favorite foods. Instead of giving in, I trained myself to simply look and smell the food before giving it away to a homeless person. Achieving this was empowering, and I celebrated my effort by sharing my success with friends and on social media.

"If you don't program yourself, life will program you!" - Les Brown

I realized that making changes in our lives can be overwhelming, but starting with just one or two good habits can make all the difference. By using them as anchors, we can keep ourselves on track and build momentum towards our goals. However, our minds can play tricks on us and try to steer us away from our new habits. That's why having anchored habits that are self-preserving and tough to disassociate from can give us the courage to push through the initial resistance.

So, allocate time and strive to make changes with good habits, and soon you'll see the benefits. Remember, anchored habits are the foundation for real transformation in our lives.

By implementing the principles of creating a new identity and visualizing it, we can hope to see several positive results, including:

Improved self-image: As you develop and reinforce a new identity, you will begin to see yourself in a more positive light and have a stronger sense of self.

Increased motivation: Visualizing yourself as the person you want to be can help to boost your motivation and make it easier to stay committed to your goals.

Enhanced focus: By having a clear vision of your desired outcome, you can more easily focus your efforts and stay on track towards your goals.

Better decision-making: When you have a strong sense of identity and purpose, it becomes easier to make decisions that align with your goals and values.

Greater confidence: As you make progress towards your goals and develop a new identity, you will likely feel more confident in yourself and your abilities.

It's essential to maintain commitment and consistency, even when our initial motivation fades away. As the saying goes, true commitment is doing what we said we would do long after the excitement of committing has passed. So, by visualizing our new identity and consistently taking small steps towards our goals, we can create lasting changes and achieve the life we desire.

Ready starters for this Chapter to start implementing:

(Scan this QR for Mental Models, Links to Proven Frameworks and Excel templates to get started)

BONUS CHAPTER

Embracing Change - A Path to Personal Growth

A tree doesn't grow half of its potential size, it soaks up everything it can to become the best version of itself. The same is not true for Humans, because we have the curse of making a choice. Reality leaves us with a choice – Pay now or Pay later. You have to pay the price nevertheless. Our daily small, seemingly inconsequential choices we make, shape our future profoundly - either good or bad ways.

Being Comfortable is a feeling of safety and physical ease, familiarity & in-control, pleasant and enjoyable. We love to live in a world of mediocrity because it's safe there. The only blessing you got is this life. Every successful person went through boring daily rituals which ultimately people noticed as one day as being blessed.

Nothing great and worthwhile in life comes easy, changing the way you look at life. It is supposed to be difficult. Don't wish if it was easier, wish you were better.

Do more of what you hate to do, it's the key to your greater success. It will be mundane and boring. To keep it easy on yourself, do it with love and joy.

Winners are those who mastered the fundamentals very well.

Luck is the macro output of hundreds of micro-actions on a daily basis.

Where your attention goes, energy flows. Energy, and not Time, is the fundamental currency of high performance. The Time spent in a state of flow gets things done.

Focus gives flow and focus comes from interval repetitions done many times over.

The world that you seek exists for real. Don't let your limiting beliefs come in the way and keep you mediocre. Never accept your current state as good enough. Don't go through life, grow through life!

The Daily routines in the 8 spheres of life often involve mundane tasks that are essential to our daily functioning. Here's a list of some of these less-than-exciting activities:

Business:

Organizing and filing paperwork, responding to emails, Tracking expenses and receipts

Finances:

Creating and sticking to a budget, Reviewing and paying bills on time

Saving money by negotiating bills or switching service providers

Relationships:

Scheduling regular check-ins with loved ones, Expressing gratitude and appreciation regularly. Setting boundaries and communicating clearly in conflicts

Physical:

Maintaining a regular exercise routine, staying hydrated and getting enough sleep

Preparing healthy meals and snacks in advance

Mental:

Practicing mindfulness or meditation, Prioritizing self-care activities, such as taking a bath or reading a book, Reflecting on personal values and beliefs

Spiritual:

Setting aside time for prayer or reflection, Reading and studying religious texts

Attending spiritual services or retreats

Family:

Creating and sticking to a family calendar for important events and activities, ensuring everyone's basic needs are met (e.g., food, shelter, clothing), Encouraging open and honest communication between family members

Lifestyle:

Cleaning and organizing living spaces, Maintaining a regular sleep schedule

Prioritizing self-care activities, such as hobbies or creative pursuits

By mastering these mundane tasks, we can free up time and energy to focus on uncomfortable but high-growth activities, such as taking on a challenging project at work, starting a new business, or pursuing a passion project. It's important to remember that growth and progress often require consistency and discipline in the seemingly small and boring tasks of daily life.

When we neglect seemingly mundane tasks, we set ourselves up for failure. Failing to do these seemingly unimportant tasks leads to missed deadlines, poor performance, damaged relationships, and even financial instability.

Are you ready to unlock your full potential and achieve greatness? Then it's time to master the mundane and conquer the uncomfortable!

You don't need to be a superstar athlete like Michael Phelps or a literary genius like J.K. Rowling to apply these principles. Ordinary people from all over the world have embraced the power of doing the boring tasks really well and facing uncomfortable situations head-on to achieve remarkable success.

Ratan Tata, who transformed the Tata Group into a global powerhouse by mastering the fundamentals of business and embracing innovation, or Malala Yousafzai, who stood up for girls' education in Pakistan despite facing life-threatening adversity.

In India, we have examples like Mary Kom, who overcame multiple setbacks and obstacles to become one of the world's greatest boxers, and Chetan

Bhagat, who went from being an investment banker to a bestselling author by stepping out of his comfort zone and embracing new experiences.

By mastering the mundane tasks and embracing discomfort, you too can achieve remarkable success in every aspect of your life.

So, what are you waiting for? Reflect on your priorities, create a routine, seek discomfort, develop a growth mindset, and surround yourself with support. These actionable steps will set you on the path to greatness and leave a lasting legacy of excellence and innovation.

Remember, the power to achieve your dreams lies within you. By doing the hard work, even when it's not glamorous, and confronting challenges with an open heart and a growth-oriented mindset, you can transform your life and make a lasting impact on the world.

So, go out there and conquer the mundane and uncomfortable, and watch as your life transforms before your very eyes.

The world is waiting for you to unleash your full potential!

Rise & Shine

I LEAVE YOU WITH SOME OF MY PERSONAL FAVORITE QUOTES:

"You can change your future as quickly as you can change your mind."

- Dr. Leland Kaiser

"I'd rather be hated for who I am, than loved for who I am not."

- Kurt Cobain

"Focus is more valuable than IQ. Discipline's more valuable than talent."

- Robin Sharma

"Concentrate all your thoughts upon the work at hand. The sun's rays do not burn until brought to a focus."

--Alexander Graham Bell

"Be stubborn about your goals, and flexible about your methods."

- Brian Tracy

"When I was 20 I wanted to be a millionaire...Now that I'm a millionaire, I want to be 20,"

- Actor and comedian Jerry Lewis

"I don't know what I think until I write it down"

- American author and journalist Joan Didion

"In God we trust, all others bring data."

W. Edwards Deming

"Humility does not mean you think less of yourself. It just means you think more of others"

- Mark W. Merril

"I hated every minute of training. But I said, 'Don't quit. Suffer now and live the rest of your life as a champion.'"

- Muhammad Ali

THE FRAMEWORK

As we come to the end of this book, I don't want to leave you with fleeting motivation that fades quickly. Instead, I want to equip you with a practical framework for lasting growth and progress.

Introducing the Making Change Happen framework - a tool that I have designed and benefitted from to great effect in my own life, with my teams, and in my coaching practice. As promised, this book is meant to be used, not just read. The success of the framework lies in application of it.

The MCH framework focuses on four key areas: Mastery, Focus, Resilience, and Discomfort. Mastery involves consistently doing the seemingly mundane tasks really well, while Focus involves being intentional and disciplined about where we direct our attention and energy. Resilience involves developing the mental and emotional fortitude to overcome obstacles and setbacks, while Discomfort involves stepping out of our comfort zones to take on new challenges and experiences.

This mental model provides a structured approach to personal and professional development that helped me and many others overcome obstacles, build resilience, and achieve their goals. By focusing on these four key areas, we can develop the discipline, adaptability, and mental toughness needed to succeed in today's rapidly changing world.

Here's a brief explanation of each component:

> **Mastery**: This refers to the skills, knowledge, and expertise you have developed in a particular area. Mastery is about becoming an expert in your field or a specific skill, which can give you a competitive advantage and open up new opportunities for growth and development. Mastery also means consistently doing the seemingly mundane tasks really well at a high level of quality and efficiency.

Focus: This is about being able to concentrate your attention and energy on the things that matter most. Focus means prioritizing your time and efforts on the tasks and activities that will help you achieve your goals, while minimizing distractions and unnecessary activities.

Resilience: This refers to your ability to bounce back from setbacks and challenges. Resilience means being able to adapt to change, learn from failure, and stay motivated and persistent even in difficult times.

Discomfort: This is about stepping outside of your comfort zone and embracing challenges and new experiences. Discomfort means pushing yourself to take on new challenges, try new things, and explore new opportunities for growth and development.

By prioritizing Mastery, Focus, Resilience, and Discomfort, we unlock our full potential and attain greater success in all aspects of life. The Making Change Happen Framework is designed for those seeking to enhance performance, overcome obstacles, and realize their full capabilities through intentional change.

Here's how the 4 quadrants look like:

Mastery	Focus
Resilience	Discomfort

Let's see how applying the Making Change Happen framework in real life looks like:

Area	Action Items	Key Results
Mastery	It's all about consistently doing mundane tasks well while developing deeper expertise in a particular knowledge area.	Achieve certification or advanced degree in the chosen area Complete a project or task that demonstrates mastery of the skill Receive recognition or promotion for the developed expertise
Focus	Prioritize tasks and activities based on their importance and impact	Complete the most important tasks first each day Minimize time spent on distractions and non-essential tasks Increase productivity and effectiveness by focusing on high-impact activities
Resilience	Develop strategies for coping with setbacks and challenges	Practice mindfulness or meditation to increase resilience and stress management Seek out feedback and constructive criticism to learn and grow from setbacks Maintain a positive attitude and keep moving forward, even in the face of adversity

Discomfort	Identify and take on challenging tasks or experiences outside of your comfort zone	Take on a new job or project that requires learning new skills or techniques Participate in a challenging activity Seek out feedback and constructive criticism to improve performance in uncomfortable situations

Here's an example of how a 'student' could apply the Making Change Happen framework:

Area	Action Items	Key Results
Mastery	Choose a subject or skill to focus on and improve in, such as math or sports while excelling in the regular tasks such as homework, punctuality, extracurriculars.	Achieve a higher grade in the chosen subject or skill Complete a challenging project or assignment that demonstrates mastery of the subject or skill Receive recognition from a teacher or professor for your improved performance
Focus	Prioritize your studies and activities based on their importance and impact	Create a study schedule and prioritize the most important assignments and exams Minimize time spent on social media and other distractions Increase productivity and effectiveness by focusing on high-impact activities, such as studying for exams or completing assignments with earlier due dates

Resilience	Develop strategies for coping with setbacks and challenges	Practice stress management techniques, such as deep breathing or exercise Seek out feedback from teachers or peers to learn from mistakes and improve performance Maintain a positive attitude and keep working towards your goals, even in the face of setbacks or difficulties
Discomfort	Take on challenging extracurricular activities or projects to expand your skills and experiences	Join a debate club or sports team to develop communication and leadership skills Participate in a volunteer project or internship to gain real-world experience and broaden your horizons Seek out opportunities to step outside of your comfort zone and learn new skills

Here's an example of how a 'job seeker' could apply the framework:

Area	Action Items	Key Results
Mastery	Identify skills or knowledge gaps and take steps to fill them.	Take an online course or workshop to develop a new skill or gain knowledge in a relevant area Seek out mentorship or guidance from someone with expertise in your field Develop a portfolio or project that demonstrates mastery of a relevant skill or knowledge area
Focus	Prioritize job search activities based on their importance and impact	Create a targeted job search strategy that focuses on the most relevant job postings and employers Customize your resume and cover letter for each job application to highlight your relevant skills & experience Network with industry professionals and attend relevant events to expand your job search opportunities
Resilience	Develop strategies for coping with rejection and setbacks	Practice positive self-talk and maintain a growth mindset, rejections and setbacks are your learnings Seek out feedback from job interviews or applications to identify areas for improvement Maintain a positive attitude and stay motivated even in the face of multiple rejections or extended job search

Discomfort	Take on challenging opportunities to expand your skills and experiences	Volunteer for a project or committee at your current job to gain new skills and experiences Attend a job fair or networking event to meet new people and improve relationship-building skills Consider applying for jobs outside of your immediate comfort zone to broaden your horizons and skillset

Here's an example of how a 'career climber' could apply the framework:

Area	Action Items	Key Results
Mastery	Identify areas of expertise and develop specialized skills	Seek out opportunities to learn from industry experts and thought leaders Take on complex projects that challenge and develop specialized skills Attend conferences and professional development events to stay up-to-date with the latest trends and technologies in your field
Focus	Prioritize tasks and projects that align with career goals	Create a strategic plan for career advancement, identifying key milestones and goals Seek out projects and opportunities that align with your long-term career goals Align your daily tasks and responsibilities with your larger career goals to maintain focus and direction

Resilience	Develop strategies for overcoming obstacles and setbacks	Practice positive self-talk and maintain a growth mindset, viewing setbacks as opportunities for learning and growth Build a strong support network of mentors, colleagues, and friends who can provide guidance and encouragement Stay motivated and focused, even in the face of unexpected challenges or roadblocks
Discomfort	Take calculated risks and seek out new challenges	Seek out stretch assignments that push you out of your comfort zone and develop new skills Take on leadership roles or mentorship opportunities to develop new perspectives and build a professional network Consider taking on a lateral move or working in a different department or role to gain new experiences and skills

Here's an example of how an 'entrepreneur' could apply the Making Change Happen framework:

Area	**Action Items**	**Key Results**
Mastery	Develop specialized skills and knowledge in the industry	Attend industry conferences and events to stay up-to-date with the latest trends and technologies Take online courses or seek out mentors to gain specialized knowledge in specific areas Collaborate with experts in the industry to expand your knowledge and expertise
Focus	Prioritize tasks and projects that align with business goals	Create a strategic plan for business growth, identifying key milestones and goals Allocate resources and prioritize projects based on their potential impact on business growth and revenue Regularly review and adjust business goals and priorities to stay focused on the most important initiatives

Resilience	Develop strategies for overcoming obstacles and setbacks	Practice positive self-talk and maintain a growth mindset, viewing setbacks as opportunities for learning and growth Build a strong support network of mentors, advisors, and fellow entrepreneurs who can provide guidance and encouragement Stay motivated and focused, even in the face of unexpected challenges or roadblocks
Discomfort	Take calculated risks and embrace new challenges	Seek out new business opportunities or markets to expand the business Take on new roles and responsibilities to expand your skillset and knowledge Consider strategic partnerships or joint ventures to grow the business and gain new perspectives

Here's an example of how the Making Change Happen framework can be used by someone who wants to join work after taking a personal break:

Area	Action Items	Key Results
Mastery	Develop or update skills and knowledge for the desired industry or role.	Take online courses or attend workshops to update technical or industry-specific knowledge Refresh soft skills, such as communication, collaboration, and time management. Seek out networking events and informational interviews to gain insights and learn from industry professionals
Focus	Clarify career goals and priorities for the re-entry process	Reflect on personal and professional goals and priorities, considering how they align with desired roles and industries Develop a targeted job search strategy, focusing on specific companies, roles, or industries that align with career goals Create a schedule or plan for the job search process, including specific actions and timelines for each step
Resilience	Build resilience and confidence to overcome challenges and setbacks	Practice self-care and stress-management techniques, such as meditation or exercise Build a support network of friends, family, or mentors who can offer

		encouragement and support throughout the job search process Stay optimistic and persistent, even in the face of rejection or setbacks
Discomfort	Embrace new challenges and opportunities to expand skills and experiences	Consider freelance or contract work opportunities to gain experience and build a network Seek out mentorship or coaching opportunities to gain insights and feedback from experienced professionals Explore new industries or roles that may offer unique experiences and opportunities for growth

Remember that mastery, focus, resilience, and discomfort are all interconnected and essential for personal and professional growth. Consistently do the seemingly mundane tasks well & further expand your knowledge area, be intentional and disciplined about where you direct your attention and energy, develop the mental and emotional fortitude to overcome obstacles and setbacks, and lastly embrace discomfort to take on new challenges and experiences for personal and professional growth. Keep these four key areas in mind and use the Making Change Happen Framework to achieve lasting growth and progress.

For the Rebel inside you: Self-talk

I may not have all the riches, but I've got the drive
Living in a big city, but I'm alive
Gadgets and cars, they don't define
My will and my heart, they're all mine
I am who I am, with audacity and courage
To fight and to win, no matter the age
I may not win today or tomorrow
But I'll get there, and have the final show
You may be smart, but I've got the will
I'll outwork you daily, and never stand still
You may win the days, but I'll win the year
The pain is a sign, my transformation is near
I'm preparing for life's match day
And on that day, I'll be ready to slay
I'm getting better every single day
My sacrifice and hard work will pave the way
I am who I am, with audacity and courage
To fight and to win, no matter the age
I may not win today or tomorrow
But I'll get there, and have the final show
Making change happen, that's what I do
No matter the obstacle, I'll push through
I am unstoppable, with my will and my might
No matter the background, I'll shine bright
I am who I am, and I'll never give in
I'll beat the odds, and in the end, I'll win.

As a first-time author, your feedback is like oxygen to me.

Scan this QR code to share your feedback about the book.

With lots of love and Metta

Dipesh

Join your tribe, register now

www.makingchangehappen.club